THE
DICTIONARY
OF
INITIALS

THE DICTIONARY OF INITIALS

BY BETSY M. PARKS

CITADEL PRESS · Secaucus, N.J.

First Edition
Copyright© 1981 by Betsy M. Parks
All rights reserved
Published by Citadel Press
A division of Lyle Stuart Inc.
120 Enterprise Ave., Secaucus, N.J. 07094
In Canada: General Publishing Co. Limited
Don Mills, Ontario
Manufactured in the United States of America

Library of Congress Cataloging in Publication Data
Parks, Betsy M
The dictionary of initials.
  1. Acronyms.   I. Title.
   PE1693.P28   423'.1   80-21910
ISBN 0-8065-0750-0

With Fond Dedication to Our **DOD** (Dear Old Dad)

FOREWORD

In our "shortcut" society, the use of initials has become a sort of second language. We reduce the name of a government agency to HUD, for example, instead of using the full name, the Department of Housing and Urban Development. We ask the pharmacist for APC to relieve our aches and pains, rather than referring to its ingredients, aspirin, phenacetin, and caffeine. Even scientists, a group not given to speaking in less-than-technical terms, refer to a Field Emission Microscope as an FEM.

Our everyday conversation contains such initialisms as MYOB (Mind Your Own Business) and VIP (Very Important Person). In baseball we speak of RBIs (Runs Batted In), and our banks are protected by the FDIC (Federal Deposit Insurance Corporation). At home we update our HVAC (Heating, Ventilating, and Air Conditioning) system and check the SAE (Society of Automotive Engineers) rating of the oil in our cars.

No matter what our occupation, education, or lifestyle, we are surrounded by the jargon of initialism. *The Dictionary of Initials* is a carefully selected collection of the most frequently used initial groups and their translations. It is designed to serve as a quick, handy reference guide for home, school, and office.

This book took nearly two years to develop because in compiling it, I tried to become immersed in a given field, then determine which initialisms comprised the most pertinent standard abbreviations within that field. Areas covered include science, technology, religion, sports, the military, transportation, finance, the arts and academia, medicine, chemicals, weights and measures, business and industry, and government.

Some listings are short, like DJ for Disc Jockey. Others are long, like SPEBQSA (look that one up for yourself). Some spell out a word indicative of their true meaning. GRUB (GRocery Update and Billing) is an example. (Incidentally, an initial group that can be pronounced as a word is called an acronym.) Some initial groups have nicknames derived from the letters. For example, FNMA (Federal National Mortage Association) is usually called Fannie Mae. And some abbreviations are historical. One such is the CCC (Civilian Conservation Corps), which is being reactivated.

Of course, new initial groups are coined constantly, so users of this book are encouraged to start their own updated lists. Space is provided for such updating at the end of the alphabetical listings.

This collection is in a sense a study of Americana, based as it is on the in languages of myriad groups of people, each group involved in its own field of expertise. I hope you will find the book not only educational, but enjoyable as well.

San Jose, California
February 6, 1980

BETSY M. PARKS

THE
DICTIONARY
OF
INITIALS

A Ampere
Angstrom
AA Aerosol Assay
Alcoholics Anonymous
Antiaircraft
Antiproton Accumulator
Artificial Aerial
Associate in Arts
Athletic Association
Atomic Absorption
AAA Acute Anxiety Attack
Agricultural Adjustment
    Administration
American Academy of Allergy
American Accounting
    Association
American Adventurers
    Association
American Arbitration
    Association
American Automobile
    Association
Arbitration As an Alternative
Army Audit Agency
AAAA Actors and Artistes of America
Associated

American Association of
Advertising Agencies

AAAL American Academy of Arts and
Letters

AAAPT American Association of
Asphalt and Paving
Technologists

AAAS American Association for the
Advancement of Science

AAB Army Air Base

AABB American Association of Blood
Banks

AAC *Anno Ante Christum* (Year
Before Christ)
Automatic Aperture Control

AACC American Association of Cereal
Chemists

AACP American Academy of Cerebral
Palsy

AACR Anglo-American Cataloguing
Rules

AACS Airways and Air Communication
Service

AACSB American Assembly of
Collegiate Schools of Business

AADC Association of American Dance
Companies

AADP American Academy of Denture
Prosthetics

AADR American Academy of Dental
Radiology

AADS American Association of Dental
Schools

AADT Annual Average Daily Traffic

AAE American Association of
Endodontists

AAF American Advertising
Federation
Antibiotics in Animal Feeds
Army Air Force

AAFC All American Football
Conference
AntiAircraft Fire Control

AAFES	Army and Air Force Exchange Service
AAFMTO	Army Air Forces, Mediterranean Theater of Operations
AAFP	American Academy of Family Physicians
AAFPOA	Army Air Forces, Pacific Ocean Areas
AAFRC	American Association of Fund-Raising Councils
AAFWS	Army Air Forces Weather Service
AAGL	AntiAircraft Gun-Laying
AAGO	Associate, American Guild of Organists
AAGP	American Academy of General Practice
AAI	Alliance of American Insurers American Association of Immunologists
AAID	American Academy of Implant Dentures
AAIN	American Association of Industrial Nurses
AALL	American Association of Law Librarians
AALS	Association of American Library Schools
AAM	Air-to-Air Missile American Agriculture Movement American Association of Museums
AAMA	American Apparel Manufacturers Association American Association of Medical Assistants
AAMC	American Association of Medical Colleges
AAMI	Association for the Advancement of Medical Instrumentation

AAMRL American Association of Medical
Record Librarians

AAMT American Association for Music
Therapy

AAMVA American Association of Motor
Vehicle Administrators

AAN American Association of
Nurserymen

AANS Advanced Automatic
Navigation System

AAO American Association of
Orthodontists

AAOO American Academy of
Ophthalmology and
Otolaryngology

AAOP American Academy of Oral
Pathology

AAP Affirmative Action Program
American Academy of Pediatrics
Apollo Applications Program
Association of American
Publishers

AAPB American Association of
Pathologists and
Bacteriologists

AAPG American Association of
Petroleum Geologists

AAPM American Association of
Physicists in Medicine

AAPMR American Academy of Physical
Medicine and Rehabilitation

AAPS American Association of Plastic
Surgeons

AAPSM American Academy of Podiatric
Sports Medicine

AAPT American Association of Physics
Teachers

AAR Against All Risks
Association of American
Railroads

AARP American Association of Retired
Persons

AARS All-America Rose Selection
Army Amateur Radio System

AAS All-America Selections
American Astronautical Society
Associate in Applied Science
AASA American Association of School
Administrators
AASHTO American Association of State
Highway and Transportation
Officials
AATCC American Association of Textile
Chemists and Colorists
AAU Amateur Athletic Union
Association of American
Universities
AAUP American Association of
University Professors
AAUW American Association of
University Women
AAV Adeno-Associated Virus
Airborne Assault Vehicle
AAVSO American Association of
Variable Star Observers
AAW Anti-Air Warfare

AB Able-Bodied (Seaman)
Aid to the Blind
Air Base
Announce Booth
Artium Baccalaureus (Bachelor
of Arts)
At Bat (Baseball)
ABA ABscisic Acid
Aerial Biosensing Association
American Bankers Association
American Bar Association
American Basketball
Association
Associate in Business
Administration
ABC Aconite, Belladonna,
Chloroform
Advance Booking Charter
Advanced Biomedical Capsule
Alcoholic Beverage Control
American Bowling Congress

American Broadcasting
Companies, Inc.
Argentina, Brazil and Chile
Aruba, Bonaire, Curaçao
(Antilles)
Associated Builders and
Contractors
Association of Boards of
Certification
Atomic, Bacteriological, and
Chemical (Warfare)
Automatic Brightness Control
ABCC Atomic Bomb Casualty
Commission
ABCD Accelerated Business Collection
and Delivery
ABE Adult Basic Education
ABEPP American Board of Examiners
in Professional Psychology
ABES Association for Broadcast
Engineering Standards
ABL Amateur Bicycle League
American Basketball League
Atlas Basic Language
ABLS Bachelor of Arts in Library
Science
American Bryological and
Lichenological Society
ABM AntiBallistic Missile
Abp Archbishop
ABP American Business Press
ABR American Bankruptcy Reports
ABS Acrylonitrile-Butadiene-
Styrene
Alkyl Benzene Sulfonates
American Bible Society
American Breeders Service
American Bureau of Shipping
ABSD Advance Base Section Dock
(Navy)
ABT American Ballet Theater
ABW American Business Women's
(Association)

ABWA American Bottled Water
Association
ABYC American Boat and Yacht
Council

Ac Actinium
Altocumulus (Clouds)
AC Alternating Current
Ambulatory Care
Anno Christi (Year of Christ)
Anodal Closure
Ante Cibos (Before Meals)
Appellate Court
Asbestos-Cement (Pipe)
Associate in Commerce
Athletic Club
Augsburg Confession
Automatic Computer
A/C Armored Car
ACA Adjacent Channel Attenuation
American Camping Association
American Canoe Association
American College of
Apothecaries
American Composers Alliance
Associated Councils of the Arts
Automatic Clinical Analyzer
ACAS Airborne Collision-Avoidance
System
ACB Advertising Checking Bureau
ACC American Corporation Cases
American Crafts Council
Atlantic Coast Conference
(Basketball)
Automatic Color Control
ACCC American Council of Christian
Churches
ACCL American Citizens Concerned
for Life
ACCUS Automobile Competition
Committee for the United
States
ACD Automatic Call Distribution

ACDA	Arms Control and Disarmament Agency
ACDC	Army Combat Development Command
ACDE	Association of Commercial Diver Education
ACDO	Air Carrier District Office
ACE	Active Corps of Executives
	Adrenal Cortical Extract
	Alcohol, Chloroform, Ether
	Allied Command, Europe
	American Council on Education
	Association for Cooperation in Engineering
	Attitude Control Electronics
ACEC	American Consulting Engineers Council
ACES	Annual Cycle Energy System
ACF	After-tax Cash Flow
	Association of Consulting Foresters
ACFM	Actual Cubic Feet per Minute
ACG	American College of Gastroenterology
ACH	Adrenal Cortical Hormone
	Automated Clearing House
ACHA	American College of Hospital Administrators
ACI	Accrued Comprehensive Income
	American Concrete Institute
	Automatic Car Identification
ACIA	Asynchronous Communications Interface Adapter
ACIR	Advisory Commission on Intergovernmental Relations
ACLANT	Allied Command, AtLANTic
ACLI	American Council of Life Insurors
ACLJ	American Civil Law Journal
ACLMRS	Advisory Committee for Land-Mobile Radio Services
ACLS	Automatic Carrier-Landing System

ACLU	American Civil Liberties Union
ACM	Abrasive Ceramic Mosaic
	Association for Computing Machinery
	Audible Current Meter
ACME	Association of Consulting Management Engineers
ACMP	Amateur Chamber Music Players
ACNA	Anglican Church in North America
ACO	American Composers Orchestra
ACOG	American College of Obstetrics and Gynecology
ACOHA	American College of Osteopathic Hospital Administrators
ACORN	Automatic CheckOut and Recording equipmeNt
ACOS	American College of Osteopathic Surgeons
ACP	Agricultural Conservation Program
	American College of Pathologists
	American College of Physicians
	Asbestos-Cement Pressure (Pipe)
	Associated Church Press
	Automatic Colt Pistol
ACPA	American Concrete Pavement Association
	Association of Computer Programmers and Analysts
ACQWL	American Center for Quality-of-Work-Life
ACR	American College of Radiology
	American Criminal Reports
	Approach Control Radar
ACRR	American Council on Race Relations
ACRS	Advisory Committee on Reactor Safeguards
	Amateur Confederation of Roller-Skating

ACS Alternating Current
Synthesizer
American Cancer Society
American Ceramic Society
American Chemical Society
American College of Surgeons
Army Community Service
Associate in Commercial Science

ACSM American College of Sports
Medicine

ACSR Aluminum Cable Steel-
Reinforced
Aluminum Conductor Steel-
Reinforced

ACT Action for Children's Television
American College Testing
Associated Container
Transportation

ACTH Adrenocorticotrophin
Arbitrary Correction To Hit
(Navy)

ACTWU Amalgamated Clothing and
Textile Workers Union

ACU American Conservative Union
Auto-Cycle Union
Automatic Calling Unit

ACUBS Association of College and
University Broadcasting
Stations

ACUTE Accountants Computer Users
Technical Exchange

ACV Actual Cash Value
All Commodity Volume
Armored Command Vehicle

ACWA Amalgamated Clothing Workers
of America

AD Accrued Days
After Date
Airworthiness Directive
Anno Domini (In the Year of the
Lord)
Anodal Duration

Athletic Director
Auris Dextra (Right Ear)
Average Deviation
A/D Analog to Digital
ADA Action Data Automation
Air Defense Artillery
American Dental Association
American Dietetic Association
Americans for Democratic
Action
Ammonia Double-Alkali
Average Daily Attendance
ADAA Art Dealers Association of
America
ADAM Advanced DAta Management
ADAMHA Alcohol, Drug Abuse and Mental
Health Agency
ADAMS Alternate Distribution And
Marketing System
ADAP Airport Development Aid
Program
ADAPSO Association of DAta Processing
Service Organizations
ADAWS Action Data Automation for
Weapon System
ADB Asian Development Bank
ADC Aide-De-Camp
Air Defense Command
Allyl Di-glycol Carbonate
Analog-to-Digital Converter
Anodal Duration Contraction
Association of Diving
Contractors
ADCs Advanced-Developing Countries
ADD Aerospace Digital Development
AD&D Accidental Death and
Dismemberment (Insurance)
ADDAR Automatic Digital Data
Acquisition and Recording
ADDRG American Deep Drawing
Research Group
ADE Association of Departments of
English

ADEA Age Discrimination Employment Act
ADELA Atlantic Community Development Group for Latin America
ADF Automatic Direction Finder
ADF-N Acid Detergent Fiber Nitrogen
ADH AntiDiuretic Hormone
ADI Area of Dominant Influence
ADIS Automatic Data Interchange System
ADIZ Air Defense Identification Zone
ADL Anti-Defamation League
ADM Admiral
Average Daily Membership
ADMA Aviation Distributors Manufacturing Association
ADOR *Angros DOs Reis* (Moon Soil)
ADP Adenosinediphosphate
Ammonium Dihydrogen Phosphate
Automatic Data Processing
ADR American Depository Recipts
Asset Depreciation Range
ADRMP Automatic Dialer and Recorded Message Player
ADS Agent-Distributor Service
American Dialect Society
AntiDiuretic Substance
Atmospheric Diving System
ADT Air Dried Ton
(Alaska) (Atlantic) Daylight Time
Average Daily Traffic
ADU Alternate Ammonium Diuranate
ADVON ADVanced echelON
ADVS Analog Design Verification System

AE Agricultural Engineer
Almost Everywhere (Mathematical)

American English
Automatic Exposure
AEA Actors' Equity Association
American Electronics
Association
American Entrepreneurs'
Association
Automotive Electric
Associations
AEAF Allied Expeditionary Air Force
AEC American Electrical Cases
Atomic Energy Commission
AECC American Evangelical Christian
Churches
AECT Association for Educational
Communications and
Technology
AEE Association of Energy
Engineers
AEEC Airlines Electronic Engineering
Committee
AEF American Expeditionary Force
AEGIS An Existing Generalized
Information System
AEI American Enterprise Institute
Average Earnings Index (Horse
Racing)
AELC Association of Evangelical
Lutheran Churches
AEMT Automatically Erectable
Modular Torus
AERA Automated En Route ATC
Automotive Engine Rebuilders
Association
AERDO Association of Evangelical
Relief and Development
Organizations
AEROSAT AEROnautical SATellite
AES American Encephalographic
Society
Audio Engineering Society
Auger Electron Spectroscopy
AESOP An Evolutionary System for On-
line Processing

Artificial Earth Satellite
Observation Program

AET Associate in Electrical
Technology

AETT Acethylethyltetramethyl-
tetralin

AEW Airborne Early Warning

AF Albumose-Free
Audio Frequency

A/F Airfield

AFA Air Force Association
American Federation of Arts
American Football Association
American Forestry Association
American Foundrymen's
Association
Associate in Fine Arts
Association of Flight
Attendants

AFAFC Air Force Accounting and
Finance Center

AFAM Ancient Free and Accepted
Masons

AFB Acid Fast Bacteria
Air Force Base
Air Freight Bill
Aluminum Four Barrel
(Carburetor)

AFBC Air Force Base Command

AFC American Football Conference
Armored Fighting Vehicle
Assumed Flow Capacity (Water)
Automatic Frequency Control

AFCA American Football Coaches
Association

AFCS Air Force Communications
Service

AFD Auxiliary Floating Dock (Navy)

AFDC Aid to Families with Dependent
Children

AFEES Armed Forces Examining and
Entrance Station

AFFA	American Formula Ford Association
AFFI	American Frozen Food Institute
AFGE	American Federation of Government Employees
AFGM	American Federation of Grain Millers
AFGWU	American Flint Glass Workers' Union
AFI	American Film Institute
	American Fur Industry
AFIPS	American Federation of Information Processing Societies
AFL	American Football League
AFLA	Amateur Fencers League of America
AFLC	Air Force Logistics Command
AFL-CIO	American Federation of Labor-Congress of Industrial Organizations
AFM	Abrasive Flow Machinery
	American Federation of Musicians
AFMAG	Audio Frequency MAGnetic
AFML	Air Force Materials Laboratory
AFN	American Forces Network
AFP	Alternative Flight Plan
	Association for Finishing Processes
AFPAC	Army Forces, PACific
AFR	Auditor Freight Receipts
AFROTC	Air Force Reserve Officers Training Corps
AFRS	Armed Forces Radio Service
AFS	American Fern Society
	American Field Service
	American Foundrymen's Society
AFSA	American Foreign Service Association
AFSC	Air Force Specialty Code
	Air Force Strategic Command
	American Friends Service Committee (Quaker)

AFSCME	American Federation of State, County and Municipal Employees
AFSWC	Air Force Special Weapons Center
AFT	Alcohol, Firearms and Tobacco
	American Federation of Teachers
	Auditor Freight Traffic
	Automatic Fine Tuning
	Automatic Fund Transfer
AFTMA	American Fishing Tackle Manufacturers Associations
AFTR	American Federal Tax Reports
AFTRA	American Federation of Television and Radio Artists
AFTS	Armed Forces Television Service
AFUDC	Allowance for Funds Used During Construction
Ag	Silver
AG	Adjutant General
	AktienGesellschaft (German Stock Company)
	Attorney General
A/G	Albumin-Globulin
AGA	American Gas Association
	American Geriatrics Association
AGAC	American Guild of Authors/ Composers
	Association of Graphic Arts Consultants
AGB	Any Good Brand
AGC	Advanced Graduate Certificate
	Amphibious Command Ship
	Associated General Contractors
	Automatic Gain Control
AGCF	Air/Ground Correlation Factor
AGD	American Gage Design
AGE	Aerospace Ground Equipment
	Associate in General Education
AGI	American Geological Institute
AGL	Above Ground Level (Soaring)

AGM	Air-to-Ground Missile
AGMA	American Gear Manufacturers Association
	American Guild of Musical Artists
AGR	Advance Gas-cooled Reactor
AGREE	Advisory Group on Reliability of Electronic Equipment
AGS	Abort Guidance System
	Aircraft Gun Sight
	Associate in General Studies
	Association of Graduate Schools
AGTOA	American Greyhound Track Operators Association
AGV	Aniline Gentian Violet
AGVA	American Guild of Variety Artists
ah	Hypermetropic Astigmatism
AH	Ampere Hour
AHA	American Historical Association
	American Hospital Association
	American Humane Association
AHAM	Association of Home Appliance Manufacturers
AHCA	American Health Care Association
AHE	Associate in Home Economics
AHEC	Area Health Education Center
AHF	AntiHemophilic Factor
AHG	AntiHemophilic Globulin
AHP	Assistant House Physician
AHR	Acier Haut Resistance (Bicycle)
AHRA	American Hot Rod Association
AHS	American Hiking Society
	American Hospital Systems
	Assistant House Surgeon
AHT	Animal Health Technician
AI	Activity Index
	Airborne Interception
	Aircraft Interception
	Amnesty International
	Artificial Insemination
	Artificial Intelligence

AIA Aerospace Industries
Association
American Institute of
Architects
American Insurance Association
Archaeological Institute of
America
Athletes In Action
AIAA American Institute of
Aeronautics and Astronautics
AIAW Association of Intercollegiate
Athletics for Women
AIBS American Institute of Biological
Sciences
AICBM Anti-InterContinental Ballistic
Missile
AIChE American Institute of Chemical
Engineers
AICPA American Institute of Certified
Public Accountants
AID Agency for International
Development
Artificial Insemination with
Donor
Associated In-group Donors
Automatic Implantable
Defibrillator (Heart)
Automatic Interaction Detector
AIDJEX Arctic Ice Dynamics Joint
EXperiment
AIDS Automated Information and
Documentation System
AIEE American Institute of Electrical
Engineers
AIESEC L'Association Internationale
des Etudiants en Sciences
Economiques et Commerciales
AIF Atomic Industrial Forum
AIH American Institute of
Homeopathy
AIHA American Industrial Hygiene
Association
AIIE American Institute of Industrial
Engineers

AIIS American Institute for Imported Steel

AIKD American Institute of Kitchen Dealers

AIM Action for Independent Maturity

Adaptive Injection Molding

American Indian Movement

AIMC Association of Internal Management Consultants

AIME American Institute of Mining, metallurgical and petroleum Engineers

AIMP Anchored Interplanetary Monitoring Platform

AIMS Automated Industrial Management System

AINA Arctic Institute of North America

AIOEC Association of Iron Ore Exporting Countries

AIP American Independent Party

American Institute of Physics

American International Pictures

AIR American Institutes for Research

Assumed Investment Return

AISC American Institute of Steel Construction

AISI American Iron and Steel Institute

AITC American Institute of Timber Construction

AITI American International Traders Index

AITU Alliance of Independent Telephone Workers

AIUM American Institute for Ultrasound in Medicine

AIW Allied Industrial Workers (of America)

AIYE Average Indexed Yearly Earnings

AJ	Ankle Jerk
	Anti-Jamming
AJA	Americans of Japanese Ancestry
AJBC	American Junior Bowling Congress
AJC	American Jewish Committee
AJE	Adjusting Journal Entry
AJM	Abrasive Jet Machining
AK	Above Knee
	Alaska
AKA	Also Known As
AKC	American Kennel Club
AKI	Anti-Knock Index (Auto Oil)
Al	Aluminum
AL	Alabama
	American League (Baseball)
	American Legion
	Arab League
ALA	American Laryngological Association
	American Legal Association
	American Library Association
	Associate in Liberal Arts
	Associate of the Library Association
	Authors League of America
ALAM	Association of Licensed Automobile Manufacturers
ALARA	As Low As Reasonably Achievable (Pollution)
ALBM	Air-Launched Ballistic Missile
ALC	American Leading Cases
	American Lutheran Church
	Assembly Language Compiler
	Automatic Level Control
ALCM	Air-Launched Cruise Missile
ALCOM	ALaskanCOMmand
	ALgebraic COMputer
ALDA	American Land Development Association
ALDEP	Automatic Layout DEsign Program

ALERT	Alternatives for Learning through Educational Research and Technology
	Automated Law Enforcement Response Team
ALF	Animal Liberation Front
ALFA	Air-Lubricated Free Altitude
ALGOL	ALGOrithmic Language
ALJ	Administrative Law Judge
ALL	Acute Lymphoblastic Leukemia
ALMA	Adoptees Liberty Movement Association
ALMC	Army Logistics Management Center
ALOA	Amalgamated Lace Operatives of America
ALP	American Labor Party
ALPA	Air Line Pilots Association
ALPAC	Automated Language Processing Advisory Committee
ALPHA	Automated Literature Processing Handling and Analysis
ALPS	Advanced Linear Programming System
	Automated Library Processing Services
ALR	American Law Reports
ALRB	Agricultural Labor Relations Board
ALS	Advanced Logistics Spacecraft
	ALuminum-Sheathed (Wire)
	American Liszt Society
	Amyotrophic Lateral Sclerosis
	AntiLymphocytic Serum
ALSC	Association for Library Service to Children
ALSEP	Apollo Lunar Surface Experiments Package
ALTA	American Land Title Association
ALU	Arithmetic/Logic Unit

Am	Americium
AM	Amplitude Modulation
	Ante Meridiem (Before Noon)
	Arithmetic Mean
	Artium Magister (Master of Arts)
	Associate in Music
AMA	Academy of Model Aeronautics
	Agricultural Marketing Act
	American Management Association
	American Medical Association
	American Minsterial Association
	American Motorcycle Association
	Automatic Message Accounting (Telephone)
	Automobile Manufacturers Association
AMAS	Automated Method Analysis System
AMB	Active Magnetic Bearing
AMC	American Maritime Cases (Law)
	American Motors Corp.
	American Music (Center) (Conference)
	Automatic Modulation Control
AMCBWNA	Amalgamated Meat Cutters and Butcher Workers of North America
AMDS	Association of Military Dental Surgeons
AME	Advanced Master of Education
	African Methodist Episcopal
	Angle-Measuring Equipment
	Average Monthly Earnings
AMEA	Africa and Middle East Area
AMET	Africa-Middle East Theater
AMEX	AMerican EXpress
	AMerican stock EXchange
AMG	American Military Government
AMI	Alternative Mortgage Instrument

American Meat Institute
AMIA American Mutual Insurance
Alliance
AMIC Analytical Methodology
Information Center
AML Acute Myeloid Leukemia
Amplitude Modulated Link
AMM. AntiMissile Missile
Associate Mercantile Market
AMNET AMerican public information
NETwork
AMORC Ancient Mystical Order Rosae
Crucis (Rosicrucian)
AMP Adenosine MonoPhosphate
Ampere
AMPAS Academy of Motion Picture Arts
and Sciences
AMPS Automated Merchandise
Processing System (Customs)
AMR Atlantic Missile Range
Automatic Meter Reading
AMS Account Monitor Service
Acute Mountain Sickness
Administrative Management
Society
Aerospace Material
Specifications
Agricultural Marketing Service
American Management Society
American Mathematical Society
American Meteorological
Society
American Microscopical Society
AMmonium Sulfamate
(Herbicide)
Anisotrophy of Magnetic
Susceptibility
AMSC Army Medical Specialist Corps
AMST Advanced Medium STOL
Transport
AMSW Master of Arts in Social Work
AMT Alternative Minimum Tax
Amplitude Modulated
Transmitter

	Associate in Mechanical Technology
	Master of Arts in Teaching
AMTRAN	Automatic Mathematical TRANslation
amu	Atomic Mass Unit
AMU	Astronaut Maneuvering Unit
AMUX	Analogue MUltipleXer
AMVER	Automatic Merchant VEssel Reporting
AMVETS	AMerican VETeranS
AMW	Average Monthly Wage
AMWA	American Medical Writers Association
AN	Acrylonitrile
	Associate in Nursing
	Axle Nut
ANA	American Nurses Association
	Army, Navy, Air force
	Association of National Advertisers
ANC	African National Congress (South Africa)
	Army-Navy-Commerce
AN-FO	Ammonium Nitrate-Fuel Oil
ANI	Automatic Number Identification
ANL	Anti-Noise Limiter
ANM	AntiNoise Modulation
ANMC	American National Metric Council
ANNA	Army, Navy, NASA, Air force measuring satellite
ANO	Air Navigation Officer (Navy)
ANPA	American Newspaper Publishers Association
ANR	American Negligence Reports
ANRC	American National Red Cross
ANS	American Nuclear Society
	Autonomic Nervous System
ANSI	American National Standards Institute

ANTA	American National Theatre and Academy
ANTU	Alpha Naphthyl ThioUrea
ANVA	American National Volleyball Association
ANVO	Accept No Verbal Orders
ANZUS	Australia-New Zealand-United States defense treaty and council

AO	Acquisition Order
AOA	Administration On Aging
	American Optometric Association
AOAC	Association of Official Analytical Chemists
AOC	Anodal Opening Contraction
	Avation Officer Candidate
AOCI	Airport Operators Council International
AOD	Argon-Oxygen Decarbonization
AOG	Arrival of Goods
AOI	Arab Organization for Industrialization
AOK	All OKay
AOP	(Air)(Armored) Observation Post
AOPA	Aircraft Owners and Pilots Association
AOQ	Average Outgoing Quality
AOQL	Average Outgoing Quality Limit
AORN	Association of Operating Room Nurses
AOS	Acquisition Of Signal
AOSO	Advanced Orbiting Solar Observatory
AOTA	American Occupational Therapy Association

AP	Abrasive Paver
	Aerosol Protective
	American Plan
	Associated Press
A/P	Authority to Purchase

A-P Anterior-Posterior
APA Administrative Procedure Act
Airline Passengers Association
American Planning Association
American Polygraph
  Association
American Psychiatric
  Association
American Psychological
  Association
AntiPernicious Anemia
Associate in Public
  Administration
APB Accounting Principles Board
Albumin Per Battery
All Points Bulletin
APBA American Power Boat
  Association
APC Aspirin, Phenacetin and
  Caffeine
Automatic Phase Control
  oscillator
APCA Air Pollution Control
  Association
APE Anterior Pituitary Extract
APEX Additive system of Photographic
  EXposure
Advance Purchase EXcursion
APF Animal Protein Factor
APGA American Personnel and
  Guidance Association
APhA American Pharmaceutical
  Association
APHA American Public Health
  Association
APHIS Animal and Plant Health
  Inspection Service
API Air Position Indicator
American Paper Institute
American Petroleum Institute
APICS American Production and
  Inventory Control Society
APL Acceptable Productivity Level

A Programming Language
Average Picture Level
APM Academy of Physical Medicine
APMEG&W Association for the Promotion of the Mathematics Education of Girls and Women
APO Army Post Office
APPA American Public Power Association
APR Annual Percentage Rate
APRAC Air Pollution Research Activities Council
APRL Alliance for the Preservation of Religious Liberties
APS American Parts System (Auto)
American Physical Society
Atomic Power Station
APSA American Political Science Association
APT Advanced Passenger Train
Alum-Precipitated Toxoid
Automatic Picture Transmission
Automatically Programmed Tool
APTA American Physical Therapy Association
American Public Transit Association
APTD Aid to the Permanently and Totally Disabled
APTIC Air Pollution Technical Information Center
APTV Associated Press TeleVision
APW Apparent Polar Wander
APWA American Public Works Association
APWU American Postal Workers Union

AQ (Accomplishment) (Achievement) Quotient
Any Quantity
AQB Army Qualification Battery
AQCR Air Quality Control Region
AQE Airman Qualifying Examination

AQL	Acceptable Quality Level
AQMP	Air Quality Maintenance Plan
Ar	Argon
AR	Arkansas
	Army Regulation
	Attainment Ratio
A&R	Artists and Repertory
ARA	Area Redevelopment Administration
ARAC	Atmospheric Release Advisory Capability
ARAM	Association of Railroad Advertising Managers
ARBA	American Rabbit Breeders Association
ARC	Action for Retarded Citizens
	American Ruling Cases (law)
	Anomalous Retinal Correspondence
	Automatic Relay Computer
ARCA	Automobile Racing Club of America
ARCS	Automated Ring Code System
ARD	Acute Respiratory Disease
ARDS	Aviation Research and Development Service
ARE	Associate in Religious Education
AREA	American Railway Engineering Association
ARENTS	Advanced Research ENvironmental Test Satellite
ARES	Amateur Radio Emergency Service
ARI	Air conditioning and Refrigeration Institute
	American Refractories Institute
ARIA	American Risk and Insurance Association
ARIES	Astronomical Radio Interferometric Earth Surveying

Authentic Representation of an
Independent Earth Satellite

ARIS Advanced Range
Instrumentation Ships

ARL Association of Research
Libraries

ARM Anti-Radar Missile
Auditing Research Monograph

ARMH Academy of Religion and Mental
Health

ARMS Accounting Resource
Management System
Asphalt Roofing Manufacturers
Association

ARNGUS ARmy National Guard of the
United States

ARP Associate Reformed
Presbyterian

ARPA Advanced Research Projects
Agency

ARPs At Risk Provisions
ARRADCOM ARmy armament Research And
Development COMmand

ARRL American Radio Relay League

ARS Advanced Reconnaissance
Satellite
Agricultural Research Service
Amateur Radio Service
American Radium Society
American Rocket Society

ARSR Air Route Surveillance Radar

ART Accredited Record Technician
Annual Renewal Term
Automatic Ranging Telescope
Automatic Reporting Telephone

ARTA America River Touring
Association

ARTCC Air Route Traffic Control
Centers

ARTOS Alternative Route To Ordained
Service

ARTS Automated Radar Terminal
System

ARU	Audio Response Unit
ARV	American standard Revised Version (Bible)
	Armored Recovery Vehicle
ARVN	Army of the Republic of Vietnam
As	Arsenic (Gray)
AS	Altostratus (Clouds)
	American Standard
	Associate in Science
	Auris Sinistra (Left Ear)
A/S	Air/Solids
ASA	Acoustical Society of America
	Amateur Softball Association
	American Scientific Affiliation
	American Society of Agronomy
	American Society of Appraisers
	American Sociological Association
	American Standards Association
ASAIO	American Society for Artificial Internal Organs
ASALM	Advanced Strategic Air-Launched Missile
ASAP	Analytical Systems Automated Purchasing
	As Soon As Possible
ASC	Accounting Standards Committee
	American Sportsman Club
	Automatic Shutter Control
ASCAP	American Society of Composers, Authors and Publishers
ASCD	Association for Supervision and Curriculum Development
ASCE	American Society of Civil Engineers
ASCH	American Society of Clinical Hypnosis
ASCI	American Society for Clinical Investigation
ASCII	American Standard Code for Information Interchange

ASCMP	Association of Second Class Mail Publications
ASCP	American Society of Clinical Pathologists
ASCS	Agricultural Stabilization and Conservation Service
	Automatic Stabilization Control System
ASCUFRO	Association of State College and University Forestry Research Organizations
ASDIC	Allied Submarine Detection Investigation Committee
ASE	American Stock Exchange
ASEAN	Association for SouthEast Asia Nations
ASEE	Advanced Semiconductor Equipment Exposition
	American Society for Engineering Education
ASF	Aniline, Sulfur, Formaldehyde
	Automotive Safety Foundation
ASFSA	American School Food Service Association
ASHA	American Speech and Hearing Association
ASHD	ArterioSclerotic Heart Disease
ASHP	American Society of Hospital Pharmacists
ASHRAE	American Society of Heating, Refrigerating and Air-conditioning Engineers
ASI	American Standards Institute
ASID	American Society of Interior Designers
ASIM	American Society of Internal Medicine
ASIS	American Society for Information Science
ASL	American Sign Language
	American Soccer League
	Army atmospheric Sciences Laboratory

ASLA	American Society of Landscape Architects
ASLR	American Short Line Railroads
ASLT	Advanced Solid Logic Technology
ASM	Air-to-Surface Missile
	American Society for Metals
ASME	American Society of Mechanical Engineers
ASMMA	American Supply and Machinery Manufacturers Association
ASMP	American Society of Magazine Photographers
ASN	Average Sample Number
ASNE	American Society of Newspaper Editors
ASNT	American Society of Nondestructive Testing
ASO	Advanced Solar Observatory
ASOL	American Symphony Orchestra League
ASP	AeroSpace Plane
	American Selling Price
	American Society of Photogrammetry
ASPA	American Society for Public Administration
ASPAC	ASian and PACific council
ASPCA	American Society for the Prevention of Cruelty to Animals
ASPO	American Society of Planning Officials
ASPT	American Society of Plant Taxonomists
ASQC	American Society of Quality Control
ASR	Airport Surveillance Radar
	American State Reports
	Automatic Send/Receive
ASS	Anterior Superior Spine
	Associate in Secretarial (Science) (Studies)

ASSC Accounting Standards Steering Committee

ASSE American Society of Safety Engineers

ASSET Aerothermodynamic/elastic Structural Systems Environmental Test

AST Advanced Supersonic Transport (Alaska) (Atlantic) Standard Time

Atomized Suspension Technique

ASTA American Sail Training Association

American Society of Travel Agents

American String Teachers Association

ASTE American Society of Tool Engineers

ASTM American Society for Testing Materials

ASTP Army Specialized Training Program

ASTRO Artificial Satellite, Time and Radio Orbit

ASTT American Society of Traffic and Transportation

ASUC American Society of University Composers

ASV Air-to-Surface Vessels

ASVAB Armed Services Vocational Aptitude Battery

ASW AntiSubmarine Warfare

at Ampere-Turn

At Astatine

AT American Terms (Marine Insurance)

Anti-Tank

ATA Air Transport Association

Alimentary Toxic Aleukia

Amateur Trapshooting Association

American Tinnitus Association

American Translators
Association
American Trucking Association
American Tunaboat Association
AminoTriAzole
Associate Technical Aide

ATAC Army Tank-Automotive
Command
ATB Aeration Test Burner
ATC After Top Center (Auto)
Air Traffic Controller
Air Transport Command
Alcoholism Treatment Center
Antenna Tuning Control
Automatic Time Correction
Automatic Train Control
ATCA Advanced Tanker/Cargo
Aircraft
ATCC American Type Culture
Collection
ATCRBS Air Traffic Control Radar
Beacon System
ATDA American Train Dispatchers
Association
ATDC After Top Dead Center (Auto)
ATE Association of Teacher
Educators
ATF Across The Fence (Real Estate)
ATGSB Aptitude Test for Graduate
Schools of Business
ATI Average Total Inspection
ATLA American Trial Lawyers
Association
ATM Automated Teller Machine
ATMA American Textile Machinery
Association
ATMI American Textile
Manufacturers Institute
ATO Automatic Train Operation
ATP (Adenine) (Adenosine)
TriPhosphate
Association of Tennis
Professionals

ATR	Anti-Transmit-Receive
ATRA	Advanced TRansit Association
ATRM	American Tax Reduction Movement
ATS	Air-to-Ship
	Alternative To Suspension
	Anxiety Tension State
	Applications Technology Satellite
	Army Transport Service
	Automatic Transfer Service (Bank)
A&TT	Alcohol and Tobacco Tax
AT&T	American Telephone And Telegraph
ATU	Amalgamated Transit Union
ATVAS	Academy of TeleVision Arts and Sciences
Au	Gold
AU	Abbreviated time Unit
	Astronomical Unit
AURA	Association of Universities for Research in Astronomy
AUSA	Association of the United States Army
AUTODIN	AUTOmatic DIgital Network
AUTOSTRAD	AUTOmated System for TRAnsportation Data
AUTOVON	AUTOmatic VOice Network
AUU	Association of Urban Universities
av	Avoirdupois
AV	Atrio-Ventricular
	Audiovisual
A-V	Arteriovenous
AVA	American Vocational Association
AVC	American Veterans Committee
	Automatic Volume Control
AVE	Automatic Volume Expansion
AVF	All Volunteer Force

AVG	American Volunteer Group
AVHRR	Advanced Very-High-Resolution Radiometer
AVIONICS	AVIation electrONICS
AVROC	AViation Reserve Officer Candidate

AW	All-Widths (Timber)
	Atomic Weight
AWA	American Wilderness Alliance
AWAC	Airborne Warning And Control
AWAN	Antisubmarine Warfare operator AirmaN
AWED	American Woman's Economic Development
AWG	American Wire Gage
AWI	Animal Welfare Institute
AWIU	Aluminum Workers International Union
AWO	American Waterways Operators
AWOL	Absent WithOut Leave
AWPA	American Wood Preservers Association
AWPPW	Association of Western Pulp and Paper Workers
AWR	Adventist World Radio
AWS	Air Weather Service
	American Welding Society
AWT	Advanced Wastewater Treatment
awu	Atomic Weight Unit
AWWA	American Water Works Association
AYC	American Youth Congress
AYD	American Youth for Democracy
AYH	American Youth Hostels
AZ	Arizona

B

B Billion
  Boron
Ba Barium
BA *Baccalaureus Artium* (Bachelor
  of Arts)
  Batting Average
B/A Beam Approach
BAs Banker's Acceptances
BAA Bachelor of Applied Arts
  Basketball Association of
  America
BAAE Bachelor of Arts in Aeronautical
  Engineering
BAB Blind Approach Beacon
BABI Basaltic Achondrite Best Initial
BABS Blind Approach Beacon System
BACAT Barge Aboard CATamaran
BADCT Best Available Demonstrated
  Control Technology
BADF Buffered Acid Detergent Fiber
BAE Bachelor of Agricultural
  Engineering
  Bachelor of Arts in Education
BAI Bank Administration Institute
BAL Basic Assembly Language

BAM	Bachelor of Applied Mathematics
	Bachelor of Arts in Music
BAO	Bachelor of Arts in Oratory
BAPCT	Bachelor of Arts in Practical Christian Training
BAPSA	Broadcast Advertising Producers Society of America
BAR	Browning Automatic Rifle
BARCAP	BARrier Combat Air Patrol
BARLAB	Behavioral Alcohol Research LABoratory
BAS	Bachelor of Applied Science
BASIC	Beginner's All-purpose Symbolic Instruction Code
BASS	Bass Anglers Sportsman Society
BAT	Bachelor of Arts in Teaching
BATEA	Best Available Technology Economically Achievable
BATF	Bureau of Alcohol, Tobacco and Firearms
BB	Base Box
	Bases on Balls (Allowed)
	Battleship
	Blocking Back
	Bullet Breech
B&B	Bed and Breakfast
BBA	Bachelor of Business Administration
BBB	Better Business Bureau
	Blood-Brain Barrier
BBC	Basic Building Code
	Before Bottom Center (Auto)
	British Broadcasting Corporation
	Brombenzylcyanide
BBD	Bucket-Brigade Device
bbl	Barrel
BBQ	Barbecue
BBT	Basal Body Temperature
BC	Bachelor of Chemistry

	Balance-Current (Electrical)
	Bayonet Cap
	Before Christ
	Bomber Command
	British Columbia
B/C	Barrel-Cocking
BCA	Business Committee for the Arts
bcc	Body-Centered Cubic structure
BCCA	Beer Can Collectors of America
BCCP	Biotin Carboxyl Carrier Protein
BCD	Binary Coded Decimal
BCE	Basal Cell Epithelioma
	Bachelor of Chemical Engineering
	Bachelor of Christian Education
	Bachelor of Civil Engineering
	Before Common Era
BCG	Bacillus Calmette Guerin
BCL	Bachelor of Civil Law
BCM	Bachelor of Church Music
BCP	Bachelor of City Planning
BCS	Bachelor of Commercial Science
BCU	Big Close-Up (TV)
BCWIUA	Bakery and Confectionery Workers' International Union of America
BCY	Bank Cubic Yard

BD	Bachelor of Divinity
	Bulk Density
BDA	Benzyldimethylamine
BDC	Bullet Drop Compensator
BDI	Brand Development Index
BDL	Basic Dead Load (Building)
BDP	Bahamian Democratic Party
	Business Data Processing
BDS	Bachelor of Dental Surgery
BDSA	Business and Defense Services Administration
BDV	BreakDown Voltage
BDWB	Bone Dry Weight Basis

| **Be** | Beryllium |

BE	Bachelor of Education
	Bachelor of Engineering
	British English
B/E	Bill of Exchange
BEA	Binary Encounter Approximation
	Broadcast Education Associations
	Bureau of Economic Analysis
BEC	Bureau of Employees' Compensation
BECO	Booster Engine Cut-Off (Space)
BEE	Bachelor of Electrical Engineering
BEH	Bureau of Education for the Handicapped
BEI	Breakerless Electronic Ignition
	Butanol-Extractable Iodine
BEIR	Biological Effects of Ionizing Radiation
BEM	Bachelor of Engineering of Mines
BEMA	Business Equipment Manufacturers Association
BEMF	Back ElectroMotive Force
BEOG	Basic Education Opportunity Grant
BEP	Bachelor of Engineering Physics
	Best-Efficiency Point
	Break-Even Point
BEPS	Building Energy Performance Standards
BEQ	Bachelor Enlisted Quarters
BER	Brainstem Evoked Response (Hearing)
BES	Bachelor of Engineering Science
beV	Billion Electron Volts
bf	Board Foot
BF	Bachelor of Forestry
BFA	Bachelor of Fine Arts
BFO	Beat Frequency Oscillator
BFP	Bona Fide Purchaser

BFPR Basic Fluid Power Research
BFS Bachelor of Foreign Service
BFT Bachelor of Foreign Trade

BG Birmingham Gage
Brigadier General
BGA Better Government Association
BGE Bachelor of Geological
Engineering
BGH Bovine Growth Hormone

BH Basal area times Height
BlastHole (Drilling)
BHA Base Housing Amount
Butylated HydroxyAnisole
BHC Benzene HexaChloride
Busy-Hour Call
BHCC Better Heating-Cooling Council
BHE Bureau of Higher Education
BHL Bachelor of Hebrew Literature
BHM Bureau of Health Manpower
BHN Brinell Hardness Number
bhp Brake HorsePower
BHPRD Bureau of Health Planning and
Resources Development
BHT Bottom-Hole Temperature
(Drilling)
Butylated HydroxyToluene

Bi Bismuth
B&I Bankruptcy And Insolvency
BIA Bicycle Institute of America
Binding Industries of America
Boating Industry Association
Building Industry Association
Bureau of Indian Affairs
BID Bachelor of Industrial Design
BIE Bachelor of Industrial
Engineering
Bureau of Investigations and
Enforcement
BIFMA Business and Institutional
Furniture Manufacturer's
Association

BIH Bureau Internationale de
l'Heure
BIL Basic Impulse Insulation
BIOS BIOlogical Satellite
BIPM International Bureau of
Weights (Poids) and Measures
BIRS Basic Indexing and Retrieval
System
BIS Bank for International
Settlements
Brain Information Service
BIT Bachelor of Industrial
Technology
BInary digiT
BITE Built-In Test Equipment

BJ Bachelor of Journalism

Bk Berkelium
BK Below Knee

BL Bachelor of Laws
Baseline
B/L Bill of Lading
B&L Building and Loan
BLA Bachelor of Landscape
Architecture
BLE Brotherhood of Locomotive
Engineers
BLI Bachelor of Literary
Interpretation
BLIP Background Limited Infrared
Photo-conduction
BLISS Basic Language for
Implementing Systems
Software
BLM Bureau of Land Management
BLR Browning Lever Rifle
BLS Bachelor of Library Science
Basic Life Support
Bureau of Labor Statistics
BLT Bacon, Lettuce and Tomato
Base Level of Treatment

BLU	Basic Logic Unit
BM	Bachelor of Medicine
	Bachelor of Music
	Bipolar Magnetic (Sun)
	Board Measure
	Bowel Movement
BMC	Bulk Mail Center
BMCS	Bureau of Motor Carrier Safety
BME	Bachelor of Mechanical Engineering
	Bachelor of Music Education
bmep	Brake Mean Effective Pressure
BMEWS	Ballistic Missile Early Warning System
BMI	Broadcast Music, Incorporated (Licensing)
BMIR	Below Market Interest Rate
BMNC	Beginning Morning Nautical Twilight
BMOC	Big Man On Campus
BMPIUA	Bricklayers, Masons and Plasterers' International Union of America
BMR	Basal Metabolic Rate
BMS	Bachelor of Marine Science
	Bacteriologic Monitoring Service
BMT	Bachelor of Medical Technology
	Basic Motion Timestudy
BMV	Brome Mosaic Virus
BMW	Bavarian Motor Works
BMWE	Brotherhood of Maintenance of Way Employees
BMX	Bicycle MotoCross
BN	Bachelor of Nursing
	Boron Nitride
BNA	Basal Anatomical Nomenclature
BNDD	Bureau of Narcotics and Dangerous Drugs
BNF	Brand Names Foundation
BNS	Bachelor of Naval Science

BNSA	Background Noise Suppression Amplifier
BOCA	Building Officials and Code Administrators
BOD	(Biochemical) (Biological) Oxygen Demand
BOF	Basic Oxygen Furnace
	Best Opening Face (Lumber)
BOLD	Blind Outdoor Leisure Development
BOM	Beginning Of Month
BOP	Basic Oxygen Process
	BlowOut Preventer (Drilling)
BOQ	Bachelor Officers Quarters
BOR	Bureau of Outdoor Recreation
BOS	Basic Operating System (Computer)
BOSS	Bomb Orbital Strategic System
BOT	Beginning Of Tape
bp	Boiling Point
BP	Beautiful People
	Before Present
	Bermuda Plan (Travel)
	Between Perpendiculars (Building)
	Blood Pressure
	Blueprint
	Bursting Pressure
B/P	Bills Payable
BPA	Bachelor of Professional Arts
BPAA	Bowling Proprietors' Association of America
B/PAA	Business/Professional Advertising Association
BPCM	Best Practical Control Method
BPCT	Best Practical Control Technology
BPE	Bachelor of Physical Education
BPH	Benign Prostatic Hypertrophy
bpi	Bits Per Inch
BPI	Brand Potential Index
BPOE	Benevolent and Protective Order of Elks

BPT Best Practical Treatment
BPTCA Best Practical Technology
Currently Available
BPW Business and Professional
Women

Bq Becquerel

Br Bromine
B/R Bills Receivable
BRAB Buildings Research Advisory
Board
BRAC Brotherhood of Railway, Airline
and steamship Clerks
BRAT Bi-drive Recreational All-
terrain Transporter
BRC Broadcast Rating Council
BRE Bachelor of Religious Education
BRI Brand Rating Index
BRIOH Bureau of Retirement,
Insurance and Occupational
Health
BROWSER BRowsing On-line With
SElective Retrieval
BRS Brotherhood of Railroad
Signalmen

b/s Bits per Second
BS Bachelor of Science
Breaking Strain
B&S Brown and Sharpe (Wire)
Bore and Stroke
BSA Bachelor of Science in
Agriculture
Botanical Society of America
Boy Scouts of America
BSAA Bachelor of Science n Applied
Arts
BSAE Bachelor of Science in
Agricultural Engineering
BSAM Basic Sequential Access Method
(Computer)
BSBA Bachelor of Science in Business
Administration

BSC	Bachelor of Science in Commerce
BSCE	Bachelor of Science in Civil Engineering
BSCP	Brotherhood of Sleeping Car Porters
BSD	Bachelor of Science in Design
BSE	Bachelor of Science in Engineering
	Breast Self-Examination
BSEE	Bachelor of Science in Electrical Engineering
BSEM	Bachelor of Science in Engineering of Mines
BSEP	Bachelor of Science in Engineering Physics
BSES	Bachelor of Science in Engineering Sciences
bsfc	Brake Specific Fuel Consumption
BSFM	Bachelor of Science in Forest Management
BSFT	Bachelor of Science in Fuel Technology
BSGE	Bachelor of Science in General Engineering
BSHA	Bachelor of Science in Hospital Administration
BSHE	Bachelor of Science in Home Economics
BSIE	Bachelor of Science in Industrial Engineering
BSIR	Bachelor of Science in Industrial Relations
BSIT	Bachelor of Science in Industrial Technology
BSJ	Bachelor of Science in Journalism
BSL	Bachelor of Sacred Literature
BSLM	Bachelor of Science in Landscape Management
BSM	Bachelor of Science in Medicine
	Bachelor of Science in Music
	Basic Stripping Method

BSME	Bachelor of Science in Mechanical Engineering
BSMT	Bachelor of Science in Medical Technology
BSN	Bachelor of Science in Nursing
BSNA	Bachelor of Science in Nursing Administration
BSOT	Bachelor of Science in Occupational Therapy
BSP	Bachelor of Science in Pharmacy Bromsulphalein
BSPA	Bachelor of Science in Public Administration
BSPE	Bachelor of Science in Physical Education
BSPH	Bachelor of Science in Public Health
BSPHN	Bachelor of Science in Public Health Nursing
BSPT	Bachelor of Science in Physical Therapy
BSR	Bulk Shielding Reactor
BSRT	Bachelor of Science in Radiological Technology
BSS	Bachelor of Secretarial Science
BSSA	Bachelor of Science in Secretarial Administration
BSSE	Bachelor of Science in Secondary Education
BSSS	Bachelor of Science in Secretarial Studies
BST&IE	Bachelor of Science in Trade and Industrial Education
BSWU	Boots and Shoe Workers' Union
BT	Bachelor of Theology Bacillus Thruingiensis Bathythermograph Boat-Tail (Bullet)
BTA	Best Time Available Board of Tax Appeals
BTAM	Basic Terminal Access Method
BTC	Bare Tinned Copper Before Top Center (Auto)

BTDC	Before Top Dead Center
BTE	Bachelor of Textile Engineering
BTE&S	Bureau of Transport Economics and Statistics
BTI	Business Tax Incentive
BTO	Bombing Through Overcast
BTRE	Broadcast-Television Recording Engineers
BTU	Board of Trade Unit
	British Thermal Unit
BTX	Benzene, Toluene, Xylene
bu	Bushel
BUN	Blood Urea Nitrogen
BUR	Built-Up Roof
BV	Balanced-Voltage
B/V	Book Value
BVA	Bachelor of Vocational Agriculture
BVI	British Virgin Islands
BVM	Blessed Virgin Mary
BW	Bacteriological Warfare
	Bandwidth
	Barbed Wire (Fence)
B&W	Black and White
BofW	Book of Worship
BWA	Baptist World Alliance
BWE	Bachelor of Welding Engineering
	Bucket Wheel Excavator
BWG	Birmingham Wire Gage
BWO	Backward-Wave Oscillator
BWR	Boiling Water Reactor
BX	Base eXchange
by	Billion Years
BYO	Bring Your Own

C

c Cubic
  Cup
C Calorie
  Carbon
  Celsius (Centigrade)
  Combat (Rations)
  Conservative
  Coulomb
  Roman Numeral 100
Ca Calcium
CA California
  Center of Activity
  Court of Appeals
CAA Cowboy Artists of America
CAAG Civil Aviation Aid Group
CAAS Community-Action AgencieS
CAAT College of Applied Arts and
  Technology
CAB Cellulose Acetate Butyrate
  Civil Aeronautics Board
CABEI Central American Bank for
  Economic Integration
CABO Council of American Building
  Officials
CACM Central American Common
  Market

CAD	Cash Against Document
	Commutative, Associative and Distributive
	Computer-Aided Design
	Coronary Artery Disease
CADAM	Computer Augmented Design And Manufacturing
CADF	Commutated-Antenna Direction Finder
CAE	Computer-Assisted Education
CAF	Confederate Air Force
CAFE	Corporate Average Fuel Economy
CAG	Carrier Air-Group (Navy)
	Computer-Aided Graphics
CAgM	Commission for AGricultural Meteorology
CAGNE	Commerce Action Group for the Near East
CAGS	Certificate of Advanced Graduate Study
CAI	Computer-Assisted Instruction
	Current Annual Increment
CAIN	CAtaloging and INdexing
cal	gram CALories
CAL	Computer-Assisted Learning
	Conversational Algebraic Language
CAM	CAtapult (Equipped) Merchant (Ship)
	Commercial Air Movement
	Computer-Aided Manufacturing
	Content Addressable Memory
	Crassulacean Acid Metabolism
CAMA	Centralized Automatic Message Accounting
CAMI	Civil AeroMedical Institute
CAMPS	Cooperative Area Manpower Planning System
CAMRAS	Computer Assisted Mapping and Records Activities System
CAP	Catabolite gene Activation Protein
	Civil Air Patrol

CAPD Continuous Ambulatory
Peritoneal Dialysis
CAPE Coalition of American Public
Employees
CAPH Colt Automatic Pistol
Hammerless
CAPM Capital Asset Pricing Model
CAPP Computer-Aided Process
Planning
CAPPA Crusher And Portable Plant
Association
CAPPI Constant-Altitude Plan-Position
Indicator
CAPS Computer-Aided Pharmacy
System
Computer-Assisted Product
Search
CAR Civil Air Regulation
Computer-Assisted Retrieval
CARD Committee Against Registration
and the Draft
CARDS Card Automated Reproduction
and Distribution System
CARE Cooperative for American Relief
Everywhere
CARIBCOM CARIBbean COMmunity (and
Common Market)
CARISMA Corrections to Applied Research
laboratory Ion Sputtering
Mass Analyzer
CAROT Centralized Autom .tic
Reporting On Trunks
(Telephone)
CARP Collegiate Association for the
Research of Principles
CARS CAble television Relay Service
CART Championship Auto Racing
Teams
Community Artists Residency
Training
CAS Certificate of Advanced Studies
Chemical Abstracts Service
Collision Avoidance System

CASB	Cost Accounting Standards Board
CASE	Clerical and Allied Service Employees
CASH	Cumulative Account Status History
CAST	Council for Agricultural Science and Technology
CAT	Celestial Atomic Projectile
	Clean Air Turbulence
	College of Advanced Technology
	Computer-Aided Testing
	Computerized Axial Tomography
	Cooled-Anode Transmitting
CATV	Community Antenna TeleVision
CAV	Combined Attributes and Variables
	Curia Advisari Vult (Court Will Deliberate)
CAVD	Completion, Arithmetic, Vocabulary, Directions (Testing)
CAVU	Ceiling And Visibility Unlimited
CAW	Channel Address Word
Cb	Columbium
CB	Carte Blanche
	Casablanca Bloc
	Centerback
	Center of Buoyancy
	Chirurgiae Baccalaureus (Bachelor of Surgery)
	Circuit Breaker
	Citizens Band
	Common Bible
	Conical Ball
CBA	Chartered Bank Auditor
	Collective Black Artists
	Conservative Baptist Association
CBAA	Council on Black American Affairs

CBBI Cast Bronze Bearing Institute
CBC Complete Blood Count
Coordinated Bargaining
Committee
CBD Cash Before Delivery
Central Business District
CBDA Carcinogenesis Bioassay DAta
system
CBE Cab-Beside-Engine
Computer Based Education
Council of Biology Editors
CBEM Computer and Business
Equipment Manufacturers
CBF Cerebral Blood Flow
CBI China, Burma, India
CBMIS Comprehensive Budget and
Management Information
System
CBMS Conference Board of the
Mathematical Sciences
CBN Christian Broadcast Network
CBNS Capitol Broadcast News Service
CBO Combined Bomber Offensive
Congressional Budget Office
CBOE Chicago Board Options
Exchange
CBOT Chicago Board Of Trade
CBR Chemical, Biological and
Radiological
CBS Central Battery Signalling
Columbia Broadcasting System
CBT Commercial Benefit Tax
CBW Chemical and Biological
Warfare
CBX Computerized Business
eXchange
CC Carbon Copy
Closing Coil
Combined Carbon
Community College
Country Club
Cubic Centimeter
CofC Chamber of Commerce

CCA	Circuit Court of Appeals
CCAF	Community College of the Air Force
CCAT	Cooperative College Ability Test
CCB	Close Control Bombing
	Convertible Circuit Breaker
CCC	Center for Community Change
	Civilian Conservation Corps
	Commodity Credit Corporation
	Concerned Citizens for Charity
	Copyright Clearance Center
CCD	Carbonate Compensation Depth
	Charge Coupled Device
	Confraternity of Christian Doctrine
	Counter Current Distribution
CCDM	Consultative Committee for the Definition for the Meter
CCDT	Calcium Carbonate Deposition Test (Water)
CCE	Consultative Committee for Electricity
	Current Cash Equivalent
CCGCR	Closed-Cycle Gas-Cooled Reactor
CCHX	Component-Cooling Heat eXchanger
CCIA	Computer and Communications Industry Association
CCIR	Comité Consultatif International des Radiocommunications (International Radio Consultative Committee)
CCIS	Common Channel Interoffice Signaling
CCITT	Comité Consultatif International Télégraphique et Téléphonique (International Telegraph and Telephone Consultative Committee)
CCLED	Constant Current Light Emitting Diode

CCMS Computer-Controlled Machinery
System
CCN Contract Change Notice
CCP Code of Civil Procedure
Communication CheckPoint
CCPA Court of Custom and Patent
Appeals
CCPR Consultative Committee for
Photometry and Radiometry
CCR Critical Compression Ratio
CCRC Combat Crew Replacement
Center
CCS Central Certificate Service
Combined Chiefs of Staff
Communication Control System
CC&S Central Computer and
Sequencer
CCT Consultative Committee for
(Temperature) (Thermometry)
Cranial Computerized
Tomography
CCTV Closed-Circuit TeleVision
CCU Cardiac Care Unit
Consultative Committee for
Units
CCW Channel Command Word
Counter ClockWise
CCY Compacted Cubic Yard

cd Candela (candle; photometry)
Cd Cadmium
CD Capacitive-Discharge
Certificate of Deposit
Constructive Dilemma
Count Down
Current Density
C&D Collection and Delivery
C-D Convergence-Divergence
CDA Command and Data Acquisition
DBAC CetylDimethylBenzyl
Ammonium Chloride
CDBG Community Development Block
Grant

CDC	Call Direction Code
	Center for Disease Control
	Code-Direction Character (Computer)
CDEC	Combat Developments Experimentation Command
CDF	Combined Distribution Frame
CDFFC	Controllable-Displacement-Factor Frequency Changer
CDM	Coalition for a Democratic Majority
CDO	Community Dial Offices (Telephone)
CDP	Certificate in Data Processing
	Common Depth Point
	Cytidinediphosphate
CDPA	Certified Data Processing Auditor
CdS	CaDmium Sulphide
CDT	Central Daylight Time
CDW	Commercial Dry basis
Ce	Cerium
CE	(Chemical)(Chief)(Civil)(Clinical) Engineer
	Close Encounters
	Combustion Efficiency
	Common Era
	Compass Error
	Corps of Engineers
	Council of Europe
CEA	Commodity Exchange Authority
	Council of Economic Advisers
CEC	Cation Exchange Capacity
	Chicano Employment Committee
CED	Committee for Economic Development
CEE	International Commission on rules for approval of Electrical Equipment
CEEB	College Entrance Examination Board

CEFIC Conseil Européen des Fédérations de l'Industrie Chimique (European Council of Chemical Manufacturers' Federations—ECCMF)
CEI Communications Electronics Instructions
Contract End Item
CEMA Council for Economic Mutual Assistance
Council for the Encouragement of Music and the Arts
CEMF Counter ElectroMotive Force
CENTAC CENtral TACtical unit
CENTO CENtral Treaty Organization
CEO Chief Executive Officer
CEP Circular Error Possible
Concentrated Employment Program
CEQ Council on Environmental Quality
CERDO Consortium of Evangelical Relief and Development Organizations
CERN Organisation Européene pour la Recherche Nucléaire (European Organization for Nuclear Research)
CERT Council of Energy Resource Tribes
CESSE Council of Engineering and Scientific Society Executives
CET Center for Employment Training
CETA Comprehensive Employment and Training Act
CEU Continuing Education Unit
CEX Cocoa EXchange

Cf Californium
CF Capacity Factor
Cash Flow
Center Fielder

Cold Fluid
Crude Fiber
CFA Chartered Financial Analyst
College Football Association
Consumer Federation of
America
CFAE Council for Financial Aid to
Education
CFAS Center For Auto Safety
CFC ChloroFluoro-Carbons
Controlled Foreign Corporation
CFE Contractor Furnished
Equipment
CFEI Consumer and Food Economics
Institute
CFF Critical Flicker Fusion
CFH Cubic Feet free air per Hour
CFI Continuous Forest Inventory
CFM Chlorofluoromethane
Cubic Feet per Minute
CFMS Computerized Financial
Management System
CFO Chief Financial Officer
CFP Certified Financial Planner
Convenant Fellowship of
Presbyterians
CFR Code of Federal Regulations
Contact Flight Rules
Cooperative Fuel Research
CFS Cubic Feet per Second
CFSTI Clearinghouse for Federal
Scientific and Technical
Information
CFT Complement Fixation Test
CFTB Central Freight Tariff Bureau
CFTC Commodity Futures Trading
Commission
CFTR Citizens For The Republic

cg Centigram
CG Center of Gravity
Coast Guard
Commanding General
Cruiser Guided

CGC	Coast Guard Cutter
CGIC	Compressed-Gas-Insulated Cable
CGL/GLT	Corrected Geomagnetic Latitude and Geomagnetic Local Time
CGPM	General Conference on Poids (Weights) and Measures
cgs	Centimeter-Gram-Second
CGS	Council of Graduate Schools
ch	Chain
CH	Congenital Hypothyroidism
CHA	Christian Holiness Association
CHAD	Combined Health Agencies Drive
CHAMPUS	Civilian Health And Medical Program for the Uniformed Services
CHAMPVA	Civilian Health And Medical Program, Veterans Administration
CHAP	Child Health Assessment Program
CHD	Campaign for Human Development Coronary Heart Disease
CHEC	Citizens Home Energy Conservation (DOE)
CHEMRAWN	CHEMical Research Applied to World Needs
CHEMTREC	CHEMical TRansportation Emergency Center
CHF	Congestive Heart Failure Critical Heat Flux
CHL	Committee for Humane Legislation
CHLOREP	CHLORine Emergency Plan
CHOICE	Cost-effective Home Ownership in an Improved Contemporary Environment
CHSS	Cooperative Health Statistics System
CHU	Centigrade Heat Unit
CHZ	Continuously Habitable Zone

ci	Cubic Inch
Ci	Cirrus (Clouds)
CI	Cast Iron
	Color Index
	Configuration Item
	Corporate Identity
CIA	Cash In Advance
	Central Intelligence Agency
	Communications Interface Adapter
CIAP	Climatic Implications of Atmospheric Pollution
CIC	Combat Information Center
	Commander-In-Chief
	Committee of Institutional Cooperation
CICS	Customer Information Control System
CID	Compound Interest Deposit
	Criminal Investigation Department (Scotland Yard)
	Cubic Inch Displacement
CIE	Commission Internationale de l'Éclairage (International Commission on Illumination)
CIEE	Council on International Educational Exchange
CIF	Cost, Insurance and Freight
CIM	Computer-Input-Microfilm
CIMA	Construction Industry Manufacturers Association
CINCPAC	Commander-IN-Chief, PACific
CINE	Council on International Nontheatrical Events
CIP	Cast Iron Pressure (Pipe)
	Cleaned In Place
CIPM	International Committee of Poids (Weights) and Measures
CIPP	Comprehensive Incomes and Prices Policy
CIR	Commissioner of Internal Revenue

CIRES Cooperative Institute for
Research in Environmental
Sciences
CIS Cancer Information Service
CISK Conditional Instability of the
Second Kind
CIU Coopers' International Union

CJ Chief Justice
Corpus Juris (Body of Law)

ck Kilogram Calories
CKD Completely Knocked Down

cl Centiliter
Cl Chlorine
CL Carload
Cathodoluminescence
Chain Link (Fence)
Chemical Laser
Civil Law
Conversion Loss
Current Liabilities
CLA Computer Law Association
CLADR Class Life Asset Depreciation
Range
CLAES Cryogenic Limb Array Etalon
Spectrometer
CLAT Communication Line Adapter
for Teletype
CLC Cost of Living Council
CLD CelluLose Derivative
Concentrated Liquor Discharge
CLEAN Commonwealth Law
Enforcement Network
CLEAR County Law Enforcement
Applied Regionally
CLEM Cargo Lunar Excursion Module
CLEP College Level Examination
Program
CLGA Composers and Lyricists Guild
of America
CLIP Cooperative Library
Information Program

CLO	Citizens for Law and Order
	CLOthing (Insulation Value)
	Concentrated Liquor Outlet
CLOB	Central Limit Order Book
CLS	Christian Legal Society
CLU	Chartered Life Underwriter
CLUW	Coalition of Labor Union Women
cm	Centimeter
	Circular Mil
Cm	Curium
CM	Cement-Metal
	Central Memory
	Congregation of the Mission
	Court Martial
CMA	Christian and Missionary Alliance
	Country Music Association
CMB	Concrete Median Barrier
CMC	Carboxymethylcellulose
	Certified Management Consultant
	Continental Motosport Club
CMCA	Cruise Missile Carrier Aircraft
CME	Chicago Mercantile Exchange
	Continuing Medical Education
CMHC	Community Mental Health Center
CMI	Cell-Mediated Immunity
	Computer-Managed Instruction
CML	Current Mode Logic
CMM	Computer-Managed Manufacturing
CMN	Common Market Nations
CMOS	Complementary Metal-Oxide Silicon
CMP	Corrugated Metal Pipe
CMPP	Computerized Mine Planning Program
CMR	Carbon 13 nuclear Magnetic Resonance
	Cerebral Metabolic Rate
	Contact MicroRadiography

CMS   Central Market System
Certified Metrication Specialist
College Music Society
Consumer and Marketing
Service (USDA)
Continuous Magnetic Separator

CMSS Council of Medical Specialty
Societies

CMT   Civil Mean Time

CMTC Citizens' Military Training
Corps

CMX   CoMmodity eXchange

CN   Change Notice
Commonwealth of Nations
Cyanogen

CNA   Chloronaltraxamine

CNC   Computerized Numerical
Control

CNEL Community Noise Exposure
Level

CNM   Certified Nurse Midwife

CNN   Cable News Network

CNO   Chief of Naval Operations

CNS   Central Nervous System

Co   Cobalt

CO   Carbonic Oxide
Carbon Monoxide
Change Order
Close-Open
Colorado
Commanding Officer
Conscientious Objector
Coupled Oscillator

C/O   Care Of

COBOL COmmon Business-Oriented
Language

COC   Certificate Of Competency

COCO Comittee On Contracting Out

COCOM COordinating COMmittee (Arms
Sales)

COCU Consultation On Church Union
(Presbyterian)

COD	Carrier On-board Delivery
	(Cash) (Collect) On Delivery
	Chemical Oxygen Demand
CODAN	Carrier Operated Device, Anti-Noise
CODSIA	Council Of Defense and Space Industries Association
COE	Cab Over Engine
COEQ	Crude Oil EQualization
COESA	Committee On the Extension of the Standard Atmosphere
COFC	Containers On Flat Car
COGO	COordinate GeOmetry
COHO	COHerent coupled Oscillator
COIN	Consumers Opposed to Inflation in the Necessities
COL	Computer Oriented Language
COLA	Cost Of Living Agreement
COLIDAR	COherent LIght raDAR
COM	Coal/Oil Mixture
	Computer Output Microfilm
COMECON	COuncil for Mutual ECONomic assistance (Communist Nations)
COMO	COMmissioned Officers mess
COMPO	Council Of Motion Picture Organizations
COMSAT	COMmunications SATellite
COMSYS	COMmunications SYStem
COMtec	COmputer Micrographics TEChnology
CONAD	CONtinental Air Defense
CONARC	CONtinental ARmy Command
CON-ED	CONtinuing EDucation
CONTU	Commission On New Technological Uses of copyrighted works
CONUS	CONtinental United States
CONVO	Coalition Of National Voluntary Organizations
COP	Coefficient Of Performance
COPA	Council On Post secondary Accreditation

COPAT	Cash Operating Profits After Tax
COPD	Chronic Obstructive Pulmonary Disease
COPE	Committee On Political Education
COPS	Communities Organized for Public Service
CORE	Congress Of Racial Equality
COS	Cash On Shipment
	Central Opera Service
COSATI	Committee On Scientific And Technical Information
COSHI	Clearinghouse for Occupational Safety and Health Information
COSMAR	Committee On Surface Mining And Reclamation
COSMIC	COmputer Software and Management Information Center
COSPA	Council Of Student Personnel Associations
COSPUP	Committee On Science and PUblic Policy
COST	Committee On State Taxation
COWAC	Council On Women And the Church
COWE	Consultation On World Evangelism
COWPS	Council On Wage and Price Stability
cp	Candlepower
cP	Centipoise
CP	Center of Pressure
	Centerpull
	Central Processor
	Chemically Pure
	Command Post
	Construction Permit
	Continental Plan
CPA	Center for the Performing Arts

Certified Public Accountant
Closest Point of Approach
CPAC Collaborative Pesticide
Analytical Committee
CPB Charged Particle Beam
Corporation for Public
Broadcasting
CPC Calling Party Control
Computer Program Components
CPCSA Coal Producers Committee for
Smoke Abatement
CPE Central Processing Element
Charged Particle Equilibrium
Chlorinated PolyEthylene
Computer Performance
Evaluation
CPG Cotton Piece Goods
CPHA Commission on Professional and
Hospital Activities
CPI Carded Packaging Institute
Central Patents Index
Chemical Process Industries
Consumer Price Index
cpm Cycles Per Minute
Cards Per Minute
CPM Certification for Purchasing
Management
Certified Property Manager
Characters Per Minute
Critical Path Method
CPO Chief Petty Officer
Conservation Plan of Operation
CPP Current Purchasing Power
CPR CardioPulmonary Resuscitation
cps Cycles Per Second
CPSC Consumer Product Safety
Commission
CPT Civilan Pilot Training
Control Power Transformer
Corporation for Public
Television
CPU Central Processing Unit

CQ	Call to Quarters
	Charge of Quarters (Army)
	Congressional Quarterly
CQR	Secure (Boating)
CQS	Composite Quotation System
CQT	College Qualification Test

Cr	Chromium
CR	Compression Ratio
	Conditioned (Reflex) (Response)
	Control Relay (Electrical)
CRA	Community Reinvestment Act
CRBS	Customer Records and Billing System
CRC	Charities Regulatory Commission
	Civil Rights Commission
	Communications Regulatory Commission
	Current Replacement Cost
CRE	Chemical Reaction Engineering
CREF	College Retirement Equities Fund
CRI	Color Rendering Index
CRL	Center for Research Libraries
CRO	Cathode-Ray Oscillograph
CROM	Control and Read-Only Memory
CROP	Christian Rural Overseas Program
CRP	Community Renewal Program
CRS	Certified Residential Specialist
	Cold Rolled Steel
	Community Relations Service
	Congressional Research Service
CRT	Cathode Ray Tube
CRV	Contact Resistance Variation
CRVA	Current Replacement Value Accounting

Cs	Cesium
CS	ChristianScience
	Commercial Standard

Conditional Stimulus
Constitutional Supercooling
Control Switch
C/S Compustat
CSA Community Services
Administration
Confederate States of America
CSB Congregation of St. Basil
CSC Civil Service Commission
Congregation of the Holy Cross
CSCE Conference on Security and
Cooperation in Europe
CSDS Comprehensive Securities
Depository System
CSE Coffee and Sugar Exchange
CSF CerebroSpinal Fluid
Colony-Stimulating Factor
Critical Success Factor
CSI Construction Specifications
Institute
CSL Control and Simulation
Language
CSM Chopped-Strand fiberglass Mat
CSMA Chemical Specialities
Manufacturers Association
CSO Chained Sequential Operation
Chief Signal Officer
Commissioners Standard
Ordinary (Insurance)
CSP Community Shelter Planning
Congregatio Sancti Pauli
(Paulist Fathers)
Corrugated Steel Pipe
CSPI Center for Science in the Public
Interest
CSS College Scholarship Service
CSSA Crop Science Society of America
CSSB Compatible Single SideBand
CST Central Standard Time
Convulsive Shock Therapy
Critical Solution Temperature
CSW Certified Social Worker

ct Carat
CT Certified Teacher
Cold Test
Commercial Television
Computerized Tomography
Connecticut
Continental Tropical (Air Mass)
Control (Transfer)
(Transformer)
Current Transformer
CTAB CetylTrimethyl Ammonium
Bromide
Commerce Technical Advisory
Board
CTAC Cable Technical Advisory
Committee
CTB Cement-Treated subBases
CTC Centralized Traffic Control
Certified Travel Counselor
Chlortetracycline
CTD Certificate of Tax Deposit
Conductivity-Temperature-
Depth
CTE Coefficients of Thermal
Expansion
CTFA Cosmetic, Toiletry and
Fragrance Association
CTM Capacity Ton-Miles
CTMT Combined ThermoMechanical
Treatment
CTN CoToN exchange
CTO Content Troy Ounce
CTP Consolidated
Telecommunications Program
CTS Center for Theological Study
Chemically Treated Steel
Communications Technology
Satellite
CTSS Compatible Time-Sharing
System (Computer)
CTV Community TeleVision

Cu Copper

	Cubic
CU	Cross-talk Unit
CUNA	Credit Union National Association
CUSSA	Central United States Ski Association
CV	Calorific Value
	Cardiovascular
	Coefficient of Variation
CVA	Cerebro-Vascular Accident
CVD	Chemical Vapor Depositon
CVP	Condenser Vacuum Pump
	Cost-Volume-Profit
CVR	Continuous Vertical Retort
CVS	Controlled Voice Switching
CVT	CardioVascular-Thoracic
CW	Continuous Wave
C&W	Country and Western
CWA	Civil Works Administration
	Communications Workers of America
CWI	Certified Welding Inspector
CWIP	Construction Work In Progress
CWO	Cash With Order
	Chief Warrant Officer
	Continuous Wave Oscillator
CWPS	Council on Wage and Price Stability
CWS	Chemical Warfare Service
	Church World Service
	College World Series
CWSP	College Work-Study Program
cwt	Hundredweight
CWTP	Comprehensive Work and Training Program
CWV	Continuous-Wave Video
cy	Cycle
CYO	Catholic Youth Organization
CZ	Canal Zone

D	Date
	Day
	Degree
	Democrat
	Died
	Roman Numeral 500
da	Deka
DA	Distribution Amplifier
	District Attorney
DAA	Data Access Arrangement
	Disaster Assistance Administration
DAB	Dictionary of American Biography
DABS	Discrete Address Beacon System
DACOWITS	Defense Advisory Committee On Women In The Services
DADI	DiAnisidine DiIsocyanate
DADPS	DiAmino-DiPhenylSulfone
DAF	Department of the Air Force
	Desert Air Force
	Dissolved Air Flotation
DAGMAR	Drift And Ground-speed Measuring Airborne Radar

DAH	Disordered Action of the Heart
DALE	Drug Abuse Law Enforcement
DALR	Dry Adiabatic Lapse Rate
DAN	Diaminonaphthalene
DAP	Double Amplitude Peak
DAPU	Data Acquisition and Processing Unit
DAR	Daughters of the American Revolution
DARCOM	Development And Readiness COMmand
DARPA	Defense Advanced Research Project Agency
DART	Defense Against Anti-aiRcraft Techniques
DAS	Differential Absorption and Scattering
DASA	Defense Atomic Support Agency
DASV	Differential Anodic Stripping Voltammetry
DAT	Differential Aptitude Test
DATO	Discover American Travel Organizations
DAV	Disabled American Veterans
DAVC	Delayed Automatic Volume Control
dB	DeciBel
DB	Defensive Back
	Delayed Broadcast
	Bachelor of Divinity
D&B	Dun and Bradstreet
dba	Doing Business As
DBA	Data Base Administrator
	Daytime Broadcasters Association
	Doctor of Business Administration
dB(A)	DeciBel (Specific Characteristic)
DBC	Denied Boarding Compensation (Airlines)
DBCP	Dibromochloropropane
DBD	Double-Base Diode

dBk DeciBels Kilowatt
DBL Data Base Language
dBm DeciBels Milliwatt
dBp DeciBels Picowatt
dBrap DeciBels Reference Acoustic
  Power
dBrn DeciBels Reference Noise
DBS Dental Biologics Standards
DBTT Ductile-to-Brittle Transition
  (Alloys)
dBv DeciBels Volt
dBw DeciBels Watt

DC Diphenylcyanorarsine
  Direct Current
  District of Columbia
  Double Contact
D&C Dilation and Curettage
DCA Defense Communications
  Agency
  Department of Community
  Affairs
DCAA Defense Contract Audit Agency
DCAS Defense Contract
  Administration Services
DCE Director of Christian Education
DCF Discounted Cash Flow
DCFB Direct Conversion Fluid Bed
DCG Dual-Cell Gravity
DCL Diamond Cut Lug
  Doctor of Civil Law
DCPA Defense Civil Preparedness
  Agency
DCR Debt Coverage Ratio
  Direct Current Restorer
DCRF Die Casting Research
  Foundation
DCS Defense Communications
  System
  Dorsal Column Stimulation
DCT Data Communication Terminal
DCTL Direct-Coupled Transistor Logic
DCV Direct Current Voltage

DD	Destructive Dilemma
	Doctor of Divinity
D&D	Drunk and Disorderly
DDA	Digital Differential Analyzer
DDB	Double Declining Balance
DDBS	Digital Data Broadcast System
DDC	Defense Documentation Center
	Direct Digital Control
DDD	Dichloro-Diphenyl-Dichloro-ethane
	Direct Distance Dialing
DDGA	DoDecylGuaridine Acetate
DDL	Data Definition Languages
	Data Description Languages
DDP	Distributed Data Processing
DDS	Dataphone Digital Service
	Direct Digital Service
	Doctor of Dental Surgery
DDT	DichloroDiphenyl Trichloroethane
DDTA	Derivative Differential Thermal Analysis
DDVP	Dimethyl Dichlor Vinyl Phosphate
DE	Defensive End
	Delaware
	Dose Equivalent
DEA	Drug Enforcement Administration
DEAPA	Diethylaminopropylamine
DECUS	Digital Equipment Computer Users' Society
DED	Diesel Engine Driven
DEDC	DiEthyl DiCarbonate
DEL	Dollar Error Limit
DEMA	Data Entry Management Association
DEPC	Diethylpyrocarbonate
DES	DiEthyl-Stilbestrol
DET	DiEthylene-Triamine
DETA	Diethelynetriamine
DEWAT	DEactivated WAr Trophy

DF Direction Finding
Doctor of Forestry
DFA Doctor of Fine Arts
DFB Distributed FeedBack
DFC Distinguished Flying Cross
DFG Diode Function Generator
DFI Development Flight
Instrumentation
DFL Democratic Farmer-Labor party
DFM Distinguished Flying Medal
Distortion Factor Meter
DFP Diisopropylfluorophosphate

dg Decigram
DG Defensive Guard
Digital
DGA Directors Guild of America

DH Decision Height
Designated Hitter
Doctor of Humanities
Dortmund Horder
DHA Dihydroxyacetone
DHL Doctor of Hebrew Literature
DHV Design Hour Volume

DI Drill Instructor (Military)
DIA Defense Intelligence Agency
DIAC Defense Industry Advisory
Committee
DIAM Data Independent Access Model
DIBs Domestic International Banking
units
DIC Dairy Industry Committee
Dependency and Indemnity
Compensation
Disseminated Intravascular
Coagulation
DID Direct Inward Dialing
DIDC Depository Institutions
Deregulation Committee
DIG Digital Image Generating
DIIC Dielectrically Isolated
Integrated Circuit

DIM	Dynamic InterModulation
DIN	Deutsch Industrie Norm (West German Standards)
DIP	Dual In-line Package
	Ductile Iron Pressure (Pipe)
DIS	Ductile Iron Society
DISC	Domestic International Sales Corporations
DISCUS	DIstilled Spirits Council of the United States
DIY	Do It Yourself
DJ	Disc Jockey
DJA	Disc Jockey Association
	Dow Jones Averages
DJD	Degenerative Joint Disease
DJIA	Dow Jones Industrial Averages
DJT	Doctor of Jewish Theology
DKA	Diabetic KetoAcidosis
dkg	Dekagram
dkl	Dekaliter
dkm	Dekameter
dks	Dekastere
DKT	DiPotassium Tartrate
dl	Deciliter
DL	Disabled List
	Dual Levers
DLA	Defense Logistics Agency
DLGS	Doppler Landing Guidance System
DLI	Defense Language Institute
DLIM	Double-sided Linear Induction Motor
DLS	Doctor of Library Science
dm	Decimeter
DM	Demand Meter
	Deutsche Mark (West German Money)
	Dry Matter (Hay)
DMA	Direct Memory Access
DMD	Doctor of Dental Medicine

Double Meridian Distances
DME Distance Measuring Equipment
Dropping-Mercury Electrode
DMF Digital Matched Filters
Dimethylformanide
DMIC Defense Metals Information
Center
DML Doctor of Modern Languages
DMMA Direct Mail Marketing
Association
DMNA Dimethylnitrosamine
DMS Doctor of Medical Science
DMSO Dimethylsulfoxide
DMSP Defense Meterological Satellite
Program
DMT Dimension Motion Time
Dimethylterephthalate
DMZ DeMilitarized Zone

dN Decineper
DNA Defense Nuclear Agency
DeoxyriboNucleic Acid
DNBA Dinitrobenzamide
DNBP DiNitrosec-Butyl Phenol
DNC Democratic National Committee
Direct Numerical Control
DNF Did Not Finish
DNI Distributable Net Income
DNR Department of Natural
Resources
Do Not Reduce
DNS Do Not Set (Printing)

DO Delivery Order
Direct Oxygenation
Dissolved Oxygen
Doctor of Osteopathy
Drop Out (Printing)
DOA Dead On Arrival
Department Of Agriculture
DOCA Desoxycorticosterone
DOD Department Of Defense
DODD Department Of Defense
Directive

DODISS	Department Of Defense Index of Specifications and Standards
DOE	Department Of Energy
	Dyspnea On Exertion
dohc	Double OverHead Camshaft
DOL	Department Of Labor
DON	Distribution Octane Number
DORAN	DOppler RANging
DOS	Department Of State
	Disk-Operating System
DOT	Department Of Transportation
	Designated Order Turnaround
	Dictionary of Occupational Titles
DP	Data Processing
	Differential Pressure
	Disabled Person
	Displaced Person
	Double Pole (Electrical)
	Dynamic Programming
DPA	Diphenylamine
	Doctor of Public Administration
DPCM	Differential Pulse-Code Modulation
DPD	Diffusion Pressure Deficit
DPDT	Double-Pole Double-Throw (Electrical)
DPH	Diamond Pyramid Hardness
	Doctor of Public Health
DPM	Doctor of Podiatric Medicine
	Downtown People Mover
DPMA	Data Processing Management Association
dpm/s	Disintegrations Per Minute/ Second
DPN	DiPhosphopyridine Nucleotide
DPR	Dozen PaiR
DPS	Distributed Processing System
	Doctor of Public Service
DPST	Double-Pole Single-Throw (Electrical)
DPT	Diptheria, Pertussis, Tetanus
DQE	Detective Quantum Efficiency

dr Dram
DR (Dead) (Deduced) Reckoning
Development Right
DRC Diminished Radix
Complementation
DRCP Dummy RipCord Pulls
DRE Doctor of Religious Education
DREO Drawing Revision Engineering
Order
DRET Direct Re-Entry Telemetry
(Space)
DREWS Direct Readout Equatorial
Weather Satellite
DRIF DRug products Information File
DRLS Drug Registration and Listing
System
DRM Drawing Room Manual
DRO Destructive-ReadOut (Memory)
DRWAWIUA Distillery, Rectifying, Wine and
Allied Workers' International
Union of America

DS Degree of Substitution
Detached Service (Military)
Doctor of Science
DSA Defense Supply Agency
DSB *Debitum Sine Brevi* (Debt
Without Writ)
DSC Distinguished Service Cross
Doctor of Surgical Chiropody
DSDD Data Systems Design and
Development
DSH Deafness, Speech and Hearing
DSIF Deep Space Instrumentation
Facility
DSM Distinguished Service Medal
Doctor of Sacred Music
DSMA DiSodium MethaneArsonate
DSN Deep Space Network
DSO Distinguished Service Order
DSR Dynamic Spatial Reconstruction
DSRV Deep Submergence Rescue
Vehicle
DST Daylight Saving Time

DSV	Deep Submergence Vehicle
	Dilute Solution Viscosity
DT	Defensive Tackle
	Delirium Tremens
DTA	Democratic Turnhalle Alliance (South Africa)
	Differential Thermal Analysis
	Dimethyl-Triazeno-Acetanilide
DTG	Differential ThermoGravimetry
DTL	Diode-Transistor Logic
DTO	Dollar Trade-Off
DTS	Diplomatic Telecommunications System
DTV	Development Test Vehicle
DUF	Diffusion Under the epitaxial Film
DUI	Driving Under the Influence
DUMAND	Deep Underwater Muon And Neutrino Detection
DUSA	Daughters, United States Army
DUV	Data Under Voice
DVM	Digital Volt Meter
	Doctor of Veterinary Medicine
DVP	Diagonal Vanishing Point (Surveying)
	Digital Voice Protection
DVR	Department of Vocational Rehabilitation
	Digital Videotape Recorder
DWI	Driving While Intoxicated
dwt	Pennyweight
DWTT	Drop-Weight Tear Test
Dx	Diagnosis
DX	Distance
Dy	Dysprosium
dz	Dozen
DZ	Drop Zone (Military)

E	East
EA	Emotions Anonymous
	Enemy Aircraft
EAA	Engineer in Aeronautics and Astronautics
	Essential Amino Acid
	Experimental Aircraft Association
EAB	Ethics Advisory Board
EAC	Eastern Air Command
EAD	Equilibrium Air Distillation (Fuel)
EAHF	Eczema, Asthma and Hay Fever
EAL	Electromagnetic Amplifying Lens
EAM	Electrical Accounting Machine
	Evangelical Alliance Mission
EAME	European-African-Middle East
EAMTMC	Eastern Area Military Traffic Management Command
EAON	Except As Otherwise Noted
EAP	Employee Assistance Program
EAROM	Electrically Alterable Read Only Memory

EAS	Equivalent Air Speed
EAT	Experiment in Art and Technology
EAX	Electronic Automatic eXchange
EB	Electronic Business
EBCDIC	External Binary Coded Decimal InterChange
EBIT	Earnings Before Interest and Taxes
EBM	Electron-Beam Machining
EBR	Electron-Beam Recording
EBS	Emergency Broadcast System
EBW	Exploding Bridge Wire
EC	Electrical Conductivity
	Ethical Consideration
	Ethyl Cellulose
	European Community
ECAS	Energy Conversion Alternatives Study
ECCS	Emergency Core Cooling System
ECD	ElectroChemical Deburring
	Electron Capture Detection
ECDT	ElectroChemical Diffused-collector Transistor
ECF	ExtraCellular Fluid
ECG	ElectroCardio(Graph) (Gram)
	ElectroChemical Grinding
ECH	ElectroChemical Honing
ECHO	Enteric Cytopathogenic Human Orphan
	Executive Council of Home Owners
ECL	Emitter-Coupled Logic
ECM	ElectroChemical Machining
	Electronic Control Module
	Electronic CounterMeasures
	European Common Market
ECMI	Economic Council of the Music Industry
ECO	Electron Coupled Oscillator
ECOA	Equal Credit Opportunity Act

ECOSH	Electronics Committee On Safety and Health
ECOWAS	Economic Community Of West African States
ECP	Engineering Change Proposal
ECPD	Engineers' Council for Professional Development
ECR	Electronic Cash Register
	Engineering Change Request
ECS	Education Commission of the States
	Environmental Control System
	Extended Core Storage
ECSC	European Coal and Steel Community
ECT	ElectroConvulsive Therapy
ecu	European Currency Unit
ED	Electrodialysis
	Emergency Department
	Ethyldichloroarsine
	Every Day
EDA	Economic Development Administration
EDB	Ethylene DiBromide
EDF	Environmental Defense Fund
EDG	Electrical Discharge Grinding
EDL	Electric Discharge Laser
EDM	Electrical Discharge Machining
	Electronic Distance Measurement
EDNA	Emergency Department Nurses' Association
EDOP	Elimination of Discharge Of Pollutants
EDP	Electronic Data Processing
EDR	ElectroDermal Response (Skin)
	Equity Dividend Rate
EDS	Electrical Discharge Sawing
	Environmental Data Service
EDT	Eastern Daylight Time
EDTA	EthyleneDiamine Tetra-acetic Acid

EDVAC Electronic Discrete Variable
Automatic Computer
EDWC Electrical Discharge Wire
Cutting
EDXA Energy-Dispersive X-ray
Analysis

EE Electrical Engineer
EEC Electronic Engine Control
European Economic Community
EEDR Effective Equity Dividend Rate
EEG ElectroEncephalo (Graph) (Gram)
EEI Electrical Engineers Institute
EEOC Equal Employment Opportunity
Commission
EER Energy Efficient Ratio
EES Energy Extension Service
European Exchange Service

EFA Eastern Finance Association
EFD ElectroFluid Dynamic
EFG Electric Field Gradient
EFI Electronic Fuel Injection
EFL Effective Focal Length
EFLA Educational Film Library
Association
EFM Electronic Fetal Monitoring
EFT Electronic Funds Transfer
EFTA European Free Trade
Association

EG *Exempli Gratia* (For the Sake of
an Example)
EGD Electrogasdynamics
EGG Educational Growth Group
EGO Eccentric Geophysical
Observatory
EGR Exhaust Gas Recirculation

EHAP Experimental Housing
Allowance Program
EHF Extra High Frequency
EHT Extra High Tension

EHV Electric and Hybrid Vehicle

EI Emotionally Impaired
Existential Instantiation
EIA Electrical Industries
Association
Electronic Industries
Association
Energy Information
Administration
EIAC Ecological Information and
Analysis Center
EIB Export-Import Bank
EIC Engineering Information
Center
EIN Educational Information
Network
Employer Identification
Number
EIR Environmental Impact Report
EIS Environmental Impact
Statement

EJC Engineer Joint Council
EJMA Expansion Joint Manufacturers
Association

EKG ElectroCardio(Graph) (Gram)

EL Electroluminescent
ELC Evangelical Lutheran Church
ELF Extremely Low Frequency
ELINT ELectronic INTelligence
ELPAVG Equity Linked life insurance
Policy with an Asset Value
Guarantee
ELS Electrostatic LoudSpeaker
ELT Electrometer
Emergency Locator Transmitter
ELV Expendable Launch Vehicle

EM Electromagnetic
Electron Microscope
Mining Engineer

EMC	Electromechanochemical
	Encephalomyocarditis (Virus)
EMF	ElectroMotive Force
	Erythrocyte Maturation Factor
EMG	Electromyo(graph) (gram)
EMH	Efficient Markets Hypothesis
EMI	ElectroMagnetic Interference
EMIT	Enzyme Multiple Immunoassay Technique
EMP	ElectroMolecular Propulsion
	Ephemerides of the Minor Planets
EMR	Educable Mentally Retarded
EMS	Emergency Medical Service
	European Monetary System
EMT	Electric Metallic Tubing
	Emergency Medical Technician
EMU	ElectroMagnetic cgs Unit
ENCONA	ENvironmental Coalition Of North America
ENDEX	ENvironmental Data indEX
ENE	Estimated Net Energy
ENI	Equivalent Noise Input
ENIAC	Electronic Numerical Integrator And Calculator
ENR	Excess Noise Ratio
ENSI	Equivalent Noise Sideband Input
ENT	Ear, Nose and Throat
EO	Electro-Optics
	Engineering Order
	Executive Order
	Exhaust Opens
EOA	End Of Address (Computer)
EOE	Equal Opportunity Employer
EOG	Electrooculogram
eoi	Exhaust Over Inlet
EOL	Economic Opportunity Loan
EOM	End Of Month
	ExtraOcular Movement

EOP	Economic Opportunity Program
	Executive Office of the President
EOQ	Economic Order Quantity
EOR	Enhanced Oil Recovery
EOY	End Of Year
EP	Estimated Position
	European Plan
	Evangelical Press
	Extended Play
	Extreme Pressure (Lubricants)
EPA	Environmental Protection Agency
EPC	Easy Processing Channel
EPCA	Energy Policy and Conservation Act
EPLF	Eritrean People's Liberation Front (Ethiopia)
EPR	East Pacific Rise
	Electron Paramagnetic Resonance
EPRI	Electric Power Research Institute
EPS	Earnings Per Share
EPSCS	Enhanced Private Switched Communications Service
EPSDT	Early Periodic Screening, Diagnosis and Treatment
EPSP	Excitatory PostSynaptic Potentials
	Extra Prime Skills Program
EPT	Ethylene Propylene Terpolymer
	Excess Profits Tax
EQ	Environmental Quality
Er	Erbium
ER	Earned Run (Baseball)
	Emergency Room
	Endoplasmic Reticulum
	External Resistance
E&R	Evangelical and Reformed (Church)

ERA	Earned Run Average
	Emergency Relief Administration
	Equal Rights Amendment
ERAM	Extended Range Antiarmor Munitions
ERDA	Energy Research and Development Administration
ERF	Epoxy Resin Formulators
ERG	Electrolite Replacement of Glucose
	Electroretinogram
ERI	Employee Relations Index
ERIC	Educational Resources Information Center
ERISA	Employee Retirement Income Security Act
ERM	Elastic Reservoir Molding
ERMAC	Electromagnetic Radiation Management Advisory Council
EROS	Earth Resources Observation Satellite
ERP	Effective Radiated Power
	Equivalent Redox Potential
ERPs	Effective Rating Points
ERS	Economic Research Service (Agriculture)
ERT	Earth Received Time
	Environmental Review Team
ERTS	Earth Resource Technology Satellite
ERV	English Revised Version (Bible)
ERW	Electric-Resistance-Welded
	Enhanced Radiation Warhead
Es	Einsteinium
ES	Education Specialist
	Emergency Stop
ESA	Ecological Society of America
	Employment Standards Administration
ESAR	Electronically Steerable Array Radar

ESCA	Electron Spectroscopy for Chemical Analysis
ESD	Electronic Smoke Detector
ESDCP	Eligible State Deferred Compensation Plan
ESE	Employee Service Expense
ESECA	Energy Supply and Environmental Coordination Act
ESI	Equivalent Spherical Illumination
ESMR	Electrically Scanning Microwave Radiometer
ESOP	Employee Stock Ownership Plan
ESP	ElectroStatic Precipitation
	Energy Saving Payback
	ExtraSensory Perception
ESPN	Entertainment and Sports Programming Network
ESR	Electron Spin Resonance
	ElectroSlag Remelting
ESS	Electronic Switching System
ESSA	Elementary and Secondary School Act
	Endangered Species Scientific Authority
	Environmental Science Services Administration
	Environmental Survey SAtellite
EST	Eastern Standard Time
	ElectroShock Treatment
esu	ElectroStatic cgs Unit
ESV	Earth Satellite Vehicle
ES&WQIAC	Effluent Standards and Water Quality Information Advisory Committee
ET	Elapsed Time
	Ephemeris Time
	Ergotamine Tartrate
ETA	Estimated Time of Arival
ETAC	Environmental Technical Applications Center
ETC	Electronic Timing Control

ETD	Estimated Time of Departure
ETE	Estimated Time En route
ETIC	Environmental Technical Information Center
ETM	Electronic Time Measurement
ETMF	Effective Time Management Formula
ETO	European Theater of Operations
ETP	Electrolytic Tough-Pitch
ETS	Educational Testing Service
	Evangelical Theological Society
ETV	Educational TeleVision
Eu	Europium
EU	Energy Unit
EUA	Energy Utilization Analysis
EUCOM	EUropean COMmand
EURA	EURopean Area
EUSA	Eighth United States Army
eV	Electron Volt
EV	Electric Vehicle
	Exposure Value (Photography)
EVA	Ethylene-Vinyl-Acetate
	Extra Vehicular Activity (Space)
EVM	Exterior Vacuum Metallized
EVR	Electronic Video Recording
EW	End Width (Boxcar)
	Enlisted Woman
EWI	Education Within Industry
EWO	Engineering Work Order
EWT	Electrostatic Water Treaters

f   Femto
F   Fahrenheit
    Farad
    Fluorine
    Fusarium resistant vilt for
      seeds
fA   Femtoampere
FA   Fatty Acid
    Field Artillery
    Fielding Average
    First Aid
    Forced Air-cooled (Transformer)
FAA   Federal Aviation
      Administration
    Free of All Average (Marine
      Insurance)
FAAAS   Fellow of the American
      Association for the
      Advancement of Science
FAC   Federal Advisory Council
FACD   Fellow of the American College
      of Dentists
FACP   Fellow of the American College
      of Physicians

FACS Federation of American
Controlled Shipping
Fellow of the American College
of Surgeons
FACSS Federation of Analytical
Chemistry and Spectroscopy
Societies
FACT Frozen food Action
Communications Team
FAD FlavinAdenine Dinucleotide
FADF Fleet Air Defense Fighter (Navy
Plane)
FADM Fleet ADMiral
FAF Final Approach Fix (Plane)
Financial Aid Form
Financial Analysts Federation
FAGO Fellow of the American Guild of
Organists
FAGS Fellow of the American
Geographical Society
FAH Federation of American
Hospitals
FAI Federation Aeronautique
Internationale
Fresh Air Inlet
FAIA Fellow of the American
Institute of Architects
International Union of Architects
FAIR Fair Access to Insurance
Requirements
FALN Armed Forces of National
Liberation (Puerto Rico)
FAMIS Financial Accounting and
Management Information
System
FANS Fight to Advance the Nation's
Sports
FAO Food and Agriculture
Organization (of the United
Nations)
FAP Federal Aid Primary (Highways)
FAQ Fair Average Quality
FAR Federal Aviation administration
Regulation

FARN Armed Forces for National
Resistance (El Salvador)
FARS Fatal Accident Reporting
System
FAS Fetal Alcohol Syndrome
Food Advisory Service
Foreign Agricultural Service
Free Along Side
FASB Financial Accounting Standards
Board
FASEB Federation of American
Societies for Experimental
Biology
FASH Fraternal Association of Steel
Haulers
FASTOP Flutter and STrength
Optimization Program
FATSO First Airborne Telescopic and
Spectographic Observatory
FAU Federal Aid Urban
FAW Fleet Air Wing

FB Fighter Bomber
Fullback
FBA Fibre Box Association
FBB Fluidized Bed Boiler
FBC Fluid-Bed Combustion
Fully Buffered Channel
FBI Federal Bureau of Investigation
FBLI Fixed Benefit Life Insurance
fbm Boardfoot
FBM Fleet Ballistic Missile
FBN Faith Broadcasting Network
FBS Fasting Blood Sugar
Flare Build-up Study (Solar)
FBW Fly By Wire

FC Fair Cutting (Brick)
Federal Cases
Fighter Command
Fixed Carbon
Forced Circulation
Full Credit

F&C   Facts and Circumstances
(Taxes)
FCA   Farm Credit Administration
Fellowship of Christian Athletes
FCC   Federal Communications
Commission
Federal Contract Compliance
Fluid Catalytic Cracking
FCCSET   Federal Coordinating Council
for Science, Engineering and
Technology
FCF   Free Cash Flow
FCI   Federal Correctional Institution
FCIA   Foreign Credit Insurance
Association
FCIC   Federal Crop Insurance
Corporation
FCL   Friends Committee on
Legislation
FCOJ   Frozen Concentrate Orange
Juice
FCP   Federally Coordinated Program
FCRA   Fair Credit Reporting Act
FCRAO   Five College Radio AstrOnomy
(Laboratory)
FCS   Farmer Cooperative Service
Fellow of the Chemical Society
Fire Control System
FC&S   Free of Capture and Seizure
FCU   Fare Construction Unit

FDA   Food and Drug Administration
FDAA   Federal Disaster Assistance
Administration
FD&C   Food, Drug and Cosmetic act
FDCDA   Food, Drug, Cosmetic and
Devices Administration
FDIC   Federal Deposit Insurance
Corporation
FDM   Frequency Division
Multiplexing
FDMA   Frequency Domain Multiple
Access

FDP	Free Democratic Party (West Germany)
FDPC	Federal Data Processing Centers
FDR	Franklin Delano Roosevelt
Fe	Iron
FE	Factor of Evaporation
FEAF	Far East Air Force
FEBs	Federal Executive Boards
FEBA	Far East Broadcasting Association
	Forward Edge of the Battle Area
FEC	Federal Election Commission
	Food Employees Council
FECA	Federal Employees Compensation Act
FEDAL	Failed Element Detector And Location
FEDAPT	Foundation for the Extension and Development of the American Professional Theatre
FED-SPEC	FEDeral SPECification
FED-STD	FEDeral STandarD
FEGLI	Federal Employees Group Life Insurance
FEHB	Federal Employee Health Benefit
FEI	Financial Executives Institute
FEL	Familial Erythrophagocytic Lymphohistiocytosis
FEM	Field Emission Microscope
FEMA	Federal Emergency Managements Agency
FEOSO	Far East OverSeas Oil
FEPA	Fair Employment Practices Act
	Far East and Pacific Area
FEPC	Fair Employment Practices Commission
FERA	Federal Emergency Relief Administration

FERC	Federal Energy Regulatory Commission
FET	Federal Excise Tax
	Field-Effect Transistor
FETVM	Field-Effect Transistor Volt Meter
FEW	Federally Employed Women
FEX	Foreign EXchange (Telephone)
FF	Filtration Fraction
	Formula Ford
	Frozen Food
	Fashion Foundation of America
FFA	Free Fatty Acid
	Future Farmers of America
FFAG	Fixed Field Alternating Gradient
FFF	Fision-Fusion-Fission
FFIEC	Federal Financial Institutions Examination Council
ffrr	Full-Frequency Range Recording
FFS	Family Financial Statement
ffss	Full-Frequency Stereophonic Sound
FFT	Fast Fourier Transform
FFTF	Fast Flux Test Facility
FFV	First Families of Virginia
FG	Field Goal
FGA	Field Goals Attempted
	Free from General Average (Marine Insurance)
FGAA	Federal Government Accountants Association
FGD	Flue Gas Desulfurization
FGIS	Federal Grain Inspection Service
FGM	Field Goals Made
FGP	Foster Grandparent Program
FHA	Farmers Home Administration
	Federal Highway Administration

Federal Housing Administration
FHLA Farmers Home Loan
Administration
FHLBB Federal Home Loan Bank Board
FHLMC Federal Home Loan Mortgage
Corporation (Freddie Mac)
fhp Friction HorsePower
FHR Fetal Heart Rate
FHWA Federal HighWay
Administration

FIA Federal Insurance
Administration
FICs Federal Information Centers
FICA Federal Insurance
Contributions Act
FICAP Furniture Industry Consumer
Advisory Panel
FICB Federal Intermediate Credit
Bank
FICC Fixed Income Consumer
Counseling
FIDCR Federal Interagency Day Care
Requirements
FIDE Federation Internationale
D'Échecs (International Chess
Federation)
FIEI Farm and Industrial Equipment
Institute
FIFO First In, First Out
FIFRA Federal Insecticide, Fungicide
and Rodenticide Act
FIM Facing Identification Mark
Fédération Internationale
Motocycliste (International
Motorcycle Federation—IMF)
Field Ion Microscope
FIMs Financial Instrument
Memberships
FINA Fédération Internationale de
Natation Amateur
(International Amateur
Swimming Federation)

FINO Federation of Independent
Nursing Organizations
FIP Forestry Incentives Program
FIPS Federal Information Processing
Standards
FIRST Federal Information Research
Science and Technology
FIS Federation Internationale de
Ski
FISA International Auto Sport
Federation
FISH Friends In Service to Humanity
FIST Federation of InterState
Truckers
FIT Fabrication, Integration,
Testing
Foreign Independent Travel
FITA Federation Internationale de
Tir à l'Arc (Archery)
FITC Foundation for International
Technological Cooperation
FIW Film Industry Workshop

FJ Flying Junior (Boating)
FJP Federation of Jewish
Philanthropies

fl Fluid
FL Flanker
Florida
Fluorite
FLB Federal Land Bank
fl dr FLuid DRam
FLES Foreign Languages in the
Elementary School
FLETC Federal Law Enforcement
Training Center
FLIP Floating Laboratory
Instrument Platform
FLN National Liberation Front
(Algeria)
FLNC Corsican National Liberation
Front

FLOC	Farm Labor Organizing Committee
FLPMA	Federal Land Policy and Management Act
FLRB	Farm Labor Relations Board
fm	Fathom
	Femtometer
Fm	Fermium
FM	Facilities Management
	Factory Mutual
	Faience Mosaics
	Field Marshal
	Fineness Modulus
	Frequency Meter
	Frequency Modulation
F/M	Food/Microorganisms (Wastewater)
FMA	Fuel Merchants Association
FMC	Federal Maritime Commission
	Final Moisture Content
	Full Metal Case (Ammunition)
FMCS	Federal Mediation and Conciliation Service
fmep	Friction Mean Effective Pressure
FMF	Fleet Marine Force
FmHA	FarMers Home Administration
FMI	Food Marketing Institute
FMJ	Full Metal Jacket (Ammunition)
FMN	Flavin MonoNucleotide
FMV	Fair Market Value
FNBR	Fast Neutron Breeder Reactor
FNLA	National Front for the Liberation of Angola
FNM	Free National Movement (Bahamas)
FNMA	Federal National Mortgage Association (Fannie Mae)
FNP	Family Nurse Practitioner
	Floating Nuclear Plant
FNS	Food and Nutrition Service
FNWC	Fleet Numeric Weather Central

FO	Field Officer
F/O	Families within Orders
FOA	Forced Oil-cooled (Transformer)
FOB	Free On Board
FOC	Free Of Charge
FOE	Fraternal Order of Eagles
FOI	Freedom Of Information
FOIPA	Freedom Of Information and Privacy Acts
FOMC	Federal Open Market Committee
FORTRAN	FORmula TRANslator
FOY	Fiber Oriented Yarn
fp	Freezing Point
FP	Focal Plane (Camera Shutter)
	Forward Perpendicular
FPA	Federal Preparedness Agency
	Free of Particular Average
FPC	Federal Power Commission
	Fish Protein Concentrate
	Flow Process Charted
	Friends Peace Committee
FPCA	Federal Post Card Application
FPERA	Fire and Police Employee Relations Act
FPI	Fixed-Price-Incentive
FPL	Forest Products Laboratory
fpm	Feet Per Minute
FPO	Fleet Post Office
	For Position Only (Printing)
FPS	Feet Per Second
	Foot Pound System
	Frames Per Second
Fr	Francium
FR	Federal Register
F&R	Force And Rhythm (Heart)
FRA	Federal Railroad Administration
	Fleet Reserve Association
FRB	Federal Reserve Board
FRC	Federal Radiation Council
	Federal Radio Commission

FRD	Federal Rules Decisions
FRELIMO	National Front for the Liberation of Mozambique
FRG	Federal Republic of Germany
FRI	First Rate Investments
FRISCO	Fast-Reaction Integrated Submarine COntrol
FROM	Field-programmable Read-Only Memory
FRP	Fiberglass-Reinforced Plastic
FRS	Federal Reserve System
FS	Factor of Safety
	Federal Specification
	Filmstrip
FSA	Federal Statutes Annotated
FSEC	Federal Software Exchange Center
FSH	Follicle-Stimulating Hormone
FSK	Frequency-Shift Keying
FSLIC	Federal Savings and Loan Insurance Corporation
FSLN	Sandinista National Liberation Front (Nicaragua)
FSN	Federal Stock Number
FSP	Food Stamp Program
FSQS	Food Safety and Quality Service
FSW	Field SWitch
ft	Foot
FT	Faience Tile
	False Twist (Yarn)
FTA	Free Throws Attempted
	Future Teachers of America
ft-c	Footcandle
FTC	Federal Trade Commission
	Foreign Tax Credit
FTCA	Federal Tort Claims Act
ftd	Fastest Time of the Day
FTE	Full-Time Employee
FTE/S	Full-Time Equivalent Student
ft-l	Foot-Lambert
ft-lb	Foot-Pound
FTM	Free Throws Made

FTO	Foreign Trade Organization
FTS	Federal Telecommunications System
FTV	Flight Test Vehicle
FTX	Field Training eXercise (Military)
FTZ	Foreign Trade Zone
FUBAR	[Fouled] Up Beyond All Recognition
FUO	Fever of Undetermined Origin
fur	Furlong
FUTA	Federal Unemployment Tax Act
FVNR	Full Voltage Non-Reversing (Motor)
FWA	Financial Women's Association
FWAA	Football Writers Association of America
FWD	Front Wheel Drive
FWPCA	Federal Water Pollution Control Administration
FWS	Fish and Wildlife Service
FWSA	Far West Ski Association
FX	Factory eXperimental (Auto) Foreign eXchange
FY	Fiscal Year
FYI	For Your (Information) (Interest)
FZS	Fellow of the Zoological Society

G

113

g-GAC

g General (Intelligence)
Gram
G Gauss
General (Audience)
Giga
Gravity (Force)
Ga Gallium
GA General Assembly
General Assistance
Georgia
Geriatric Authority
Gibberellic Acid
Graduate Assistant
GAA Gay Activists Alliance
GAAC Graduate Admissions
Assistance Center
GAAFR Governmental Accounting,
Auditing and Financial
Reporting
GAAP Generally Accepted Accounting
Principles
GAAS Generally Accepted Accounting
Standards
GABA Gamma-AminoButyric Acid
GAC Granular Activated Carbon

GAESDA	Graphic Arts Equipment and Supply Dealers Association
gal	Gallon
GAM	Guided Aircraft Missile
GAMA	Gas Appliance Manufacturers Association
	General Aviation Manufacturers Association
GAO	General Accounting Office
GAPA	Ground-to-Air Pilotless Aircraft
GAR	Grand Army of the Republic
	Guided Aircraft Rocket
GARP	Global Atmospheric Research Program
GAS	Goal Attainment Scaling
GASH	Guanidine Aluminum Sulphate Hexahydrate
GASP	Group Against Smoking Pollution
GAT	Generalized Algebraic Translator
GATB	General Aptitude Test Battery
GATT	General Agreement on Tariffs and Trade
Gb	Gilbert
GB	Gall Bladder
GBBA	Glass Bottle Blowers Association
GBC	Ground Based Computer
GBS	George Bernard Shaw
	Government Bureau of Standards
GC	Gigacycle
G&C	Guidance and Control
GCA	Ground-Controlled Approach (Plane)
	Gun Control Act
GCD	Greatest Common Divisor
GCF	Greatest Common Factor
GCFR	Gas-Cooled Fast Reactor
GCIAA	Granite Cutters' International Association of America

GCM	Glazed Ceramic Mosaic
GCMA	Government Contract Management Association
GCMS	Gas Chromatograph Mass Spectrometer
GCR	General Council Regulations
GCS	Gate-Controlled Switch (Computer)
GCSC	Guidance Control and Sequencing Computer
GCT	General Classification Test
GCW	Gross Combination Weight
Gd	Gadolinium
GD	General Delivery
	Ground Detector
GDF	Guyanese Defense Force
GDL	GasDynamic Laser
GDMS	Generalized Data Management System
GDP	Gross Domestic Product
	Guanosinediphosphate
GDR	German Democratic Republic
Ge	Germanium
GE	Greater than or Equal to
GEA	Gas Evolution Analysis
GED	Gasoline Engine Driven
	General Educational Development (Test)
GEDP	Gross Enterprise Domestic Product
GEF	Gravel Equivalent Factor
GEICO	Government Employees Insurance COmpany
GEK	Geomagnetic ElectroKinetograph
GEM	Ground Effect Machine
GEO	Geosynchronous Equatorial Orbit
GEODES	Ground-based Electro-Optical DEep space Surveillance
GEOS	Geodynamic Experimental Ocean Satellite

GES	Green Extension System (Traffic Signal)
GET	Ground Elapsed Time
GeV	Giga-Electron-Volt
GEX	Gas EXchange
G/F	Genera within Families
GFCI	Ground-Fault Circuit Interrupter
GFE	Government Furnished Equipment
GFI	Ground-Fault Interrupter
GFR	Glomerular Filtration Rate
GFWC	General Federation of Women's Clubs
GGPA	Graduate Grade Point Average
GGS	Gravity Gradient Stabilization
GHA	Greenwich Hour Angle
	Group Health Association
GHE	Ground Handling Equipment
GHQ	General HeadQuarters
GHz	GigaHertz
gi	Gill
GI	Galvanized Iron
	Gastrointestinal
	Glazed Interior (Title)
	Government Issue
GIA	Gemological Institute of America
GIGO	Garbage In, Garbage Out
GIM	Gross Income Multiplier
GIPSY	General Information Processing SYstem
GIS	General Information System
GIT	Group Inclusive Tour
Gl	Glucinum
GL	Gun-Laying
GLA	Gross Leasable Area
GLC	Gas-Liquid Chromatography
GLCM	Ground-Launched Cruise Missle

GLM	Graduated-Length Method
GLOTRAC	GLObal TRACking
GLR	Great Lakes Rules (Boating)
GM	General Manager
	Geometric Mean
	Guided Missile
GMA	Grocery Manufacturers of America
GMAT	Graduate Management Admission Test
GML	Glycerol MonoLaurate
GMP	Good Manufacturing Practice
GMT	Greenwich Mean Time
GMW	Gram Molecular Weight
GN	Graduate Nurse
	Grand National
GNI	Gross National Income
GNMA	Government National Mortgage Association (Ginnie Mae)
GNP	Gross National Product
GO	General Order
GOE	Geostationary Operational Environmental satellite
GOP	Grand Old Party (Republican)
GOX	Gaseous OXygen
GP	General Practitioner
	Grand Prix
	Ground-Proctective (Electrical)
	Gunmakers Proof
GPA	Grade Point Average
GPC	Gel Permeation Chromatography
GPD	Gallons Per Day
GPDA	Grand Prix Drivers' Association
GP/DC	General Purpose Digital Computer
GPH	Gallons Per Hour
GPI	Glucose Phosphate Isomerase
	Grand Prix International
	Ground Position Indicator

GPL	General Price-Level
gpm	Grams Per Mile
GPM	Gallons Per Minute
	Graduated Payment Mortgage
GPO	Government Printing Office
GPP	General Purchasing Power
gpr	Gas Production Rate
GPS	Gallons Per Second
	Global Positioning System
	Groups of Pulses per Second
GPSSM	General Purpose Surface-to-Surface Missile
GQ	General Quarters
gr	Grain
GRAN	Global Rescue AlertingNetwork (Shipwreck)
GRAS	Generally Recognized As Safe
GRE	Graduate Records Examination
GRP	Glass-Reinforced Plastic
GRS	General Revenue Sharing
GRUB	GRocery Update and Billing
GS	Giant Slalom (Skiing)
G&S	Gilbert and Sullivan
GSA	General Services Administration
	Geological Society of America
	Girl Scouts of America
GSC	General Staff Corps
GSCFM	Graduate School of Credit and Financial Management
GSG	Galvanized Sheet Gage
GSLP	Guaranteed Student Loan Program
GSO	General Staff Officer
GSOP	General Stock Ownership Plan
GSP	Gross State Product
GSR	Galvanic Skin Response
GSS	Global Surveillance System
GSV	Guided Space Vehicle
GSW	Ground Saucer Watch
	GunShot Wound

gt Gutta
GT GalactosylTransferase
isoenzyme
Gran Turismo (Grand Touring;
Automobiles)
GTAW Gas Tungsten-Arc Welding
GTC Good Till Cancelled
GTT Glucose Tolerance Test
Group Timing Technique
GTW Gross Train Weight

GU Genitourinary

GVC Glazed Vitrified Clay
GVH Graft-Versus-Host
GVW Gross Vehicle Weight
GVWR Gross Vehicle Weight Rating

GW Glazed Weatherproof (Tile)
Guided Weapon
GWE Global Weather Experiment
GWP Gross World Product

Gy Gray

h	Hecto
	Height
H	Henry
	High
	Hot
	Hydrogen
HAAT	Height Above Average Terrain (Antenna)
HABA	Health And Beauty Aids
HABS	Historic American Building Survey
HAD	Half-Amplitude Duration
HAL	Heuristically programmed ALgorithmic computer
HALO	High Altidude, Low Opening (Parachute)
HAND	Have A Nice Day
HANES	Health And Nutrition Examination Survey
HAO	High Altitude Observatory
HARM	High-speed Anti-Radiation Missile
HAS	Hospital Administrative Services
HAVE	Homemaking And Volunteer Experience

HAWK	Homing All the Way Killer
HAZ	Heat Affected Zone
hb	Hemoglobin
HB	Half Back
	Heavy Bomber
HBA	Highway Beautification Act
HBPA	Horsemen's Benevolent and Protective Association
HC	Hairy Cell (Leukemia)
	High Compression
	HydroCarbon
HCA	Hexachloroacetone (Herbicide)
HCC	High-Current Configuration
HCCA	Horseless Carriage Club of America
HCDA	Housing and Community Development Act
HCFA	Health Care Financing Administration
HCG	Human Chorionic Gonadotrophin
HCI	Hospital Cost Index
HCL	HydroChLoric acid
HCN	Hydrogen CyaNide
HCR	Host-Cell Reactivation
HCRS	Heritage Conservation and Recreation Service
HD	Harmonic Distortion
	High Density (Cotton)
	Honorable Discharge
	Huntington's Disease
HDs	Head Detectors
HDL	High Density Lipoprotein
HDM	Humic Degradation Matter
	HydroDynamic Machining
HDO	Hydrogen-Deuterium-Oxygen
He	Helium
HE	High Explosive
HEAO	High Energy Astronomy Observatory

HEED	High-Energy Electron Diffraction
HEF	High Energy Fuel
HEFA	Higher Education Facilities Act
HEI	High Energy Ignition
HEL	High-Energy Laser
HELP	Heat Escape Lessening Posture
HEM	Hybrid ElectroMagnetic wave
HEOD	Hexachloro-Epoxy-Octahydro-enDo
HERF	High-Energy-Rate Forming (Metals)
HERO	Historical Evaluation and Research Organization
HES	High Early Strength
HETP	Height Equivalent of Theoretical Plate
HETS	Height Equivalent to a Theoretical Stage
HEW	Health, Education and Welfare
Hf	Hafnium
HF	High Frequency
	Hydrogen Fluoride
HFCS	High Fructose Corn Syrup
HFE	Human Factors Engineering
HFR	Hold For Release
HFS	Human Factors Society
HFW	Hole Full of Water (Drilling)
hg	Hectogram
Hg	Mercury
HG	Hemoglobin
HGF	HyperGlycemic Factor
HGH	Human Growth Hormone
HGMS	High-Gradient Magnetic Separation
HGV	Heavy Goods Vehicle
hh	Hand Height
HH	His Holiness (The Pope)
hhd	Hogshead
HHD	Doctor of Humanities
HHF	Hyper High Frequency

HHFA	Housing and Home Finance Agency
HHS	Health and Human Services
HHV	High Heat Value

HI	Hawaii
	Hospital Insurance
HIAA	Health Insurance Association of America
HIB	High Iron Briquetting
HIC	Hybrid Integrated Circuit
HIG	Hermetic Integrating Gyroscope
HIN	Hull Identifying Number
HIP	Hot Isostatic Pressing
HIPO	Hierarchical Input-Process-Output
HKD	HydroKinetic Drive
hl	Hectoliter
HL	Hooded Lever
HLF	Heart and Lung Foundation
HLH	Heavy Lift Helicopter
HLSE	High-Level Single-Ended
hm	Hectometer
HM	His (Her) Majesty
HMC	Heroin, Morphine and Cocaine
	Hospital and other Medical Care services
HMF	Hum Modulation Factor
HMM	Heavy MeroMyosin
HMO	Health Maintenance Organization
	Heart Minute Output
HMP	Hexose MonoPhosphate
HMS	His (Her) Majesty's (Service) (Ship)
HMU	Hand-Made Unglazed
HN	Head Nurse
HNS	Holy Name Society
Ho	Holmium

HO	Home Office
	Home Owner
	Hydrographic Office
HOAP	Home Ownership Assistance
	Program
HOB	Hot Ore Briquetting
HOL	Hold On Line
HOLC	Home Owners Loan Corporation
HOME	Home Oriented Maternity
	Experience
HOV	High Occupancy Vehicle
HOW	Home Owners Warranty
HP	Heat Penetration
	Horsepower
	Hydrated Protons
HPA	High-Powered Amplifer
HPB	High Performance Bank
hpf	High-Power Field
HPF	Highest Possible Frequency
	Human Powered Flight
HPGC	Heading Per GyroCompass
HPLC	High Performance Liquid
	Chromatography
HPOF	High-Pressure Oil-Filled (Cable)
HPRR	High-Performance Research
	Reactor
HQ	Headquarters
	Hydroquinone
hr	Hour
HR	High-range Radar
	Home Run
	House of Representatives
HRA	Health Resources
	Administration
HRB	Highway Research Board
HREBIU	Hotel and Restaurant
	Employees and Bartenders
	International Union
HRH	His (Her) Royal Highness
HRI	Hotel, Restaurant and
	Institution

HRIS	Highway Research Information Service
HRM	Human Resources Management
HRPRAS	High-Risk, People-Related Accident Syndrome
HRR	Heart Rate Reserve
HRS	Hard Red Spring (Wheat)
HS	Higher-Solids
	Hyperthetical Syllogism
HSA	Health Systems Agency
HSAA	Health Science Advancement Award
	High School Athletic Association
HSCI	Hospital Service Charge Index
HSI	Horizontal Situation Indicator
HSLA	High-Strength Low-Alloy (Steel)
HSP	Hollow Soft Point (Bullet)
HSR	High Speed Reader
HST	Hawaii Standard Time
	HyperSonic Transport
HSV	Herpes Simplex Virus
HT	High Tenacity (Rope)
	High Tension
	Horizontal Tube
	Hybrid Teas (Roses)
	Hydro Therapy
HTAH	High Temperature Air Heater
HTI	High-Temperature Insulating
HTL	High-Threshold Logic
HTO	Hydrogen-Tritium-Oxygen
HTPN	Home Total Parenteral Nutrition
HTPP	Hydro Thermal Power Program
HTS	HumanTissue Stimulator
HTST	High-Temperature Short-Time
HTTMT	High-Temperature ThermoMechanical Treatment
HTU	Height of Transfer Unit
HUC-JIR	Hebrew Union College-Jewish Institute of Religion

HUD Housing and Urban
        Development
HUR Homes Using Radio
HUT Homes Using Television

HVAC Heating, Ventilating and Air
        Conditioning
HVAR High Velocity Aircraft Rocket
HVD HydroViscous Drive
HVDC High-Voltage Direct-Current
HVEM High-Voltage Electron
        Microscope
HVF High Velocity Forming
HVL Half Value Layer
HVP Hydrolyzed Vegetable Protein

HW High Water
HWBA High Water BAse fluid
HWF&C High Water at Full and Change
        (Of Moon)

Hz Hertz

I	Iodine
	Roman Numeral 1
IA	Iowa
IAA	International Academy of Astronautics
IAAF	International Amateur Athletic Federation
IABSOIW	International Association of Bridge, Structural and Ornamental Iron Workers
IAC	International Athletes' Club
IACP	International Association of Chiefs of Police
IADB	Inter-American Defense Board
IAF	International Astronautical Federation
IAFF	International Association of Fire Fighters
IAG	International Association of Geodesy
IAHFIAW	International Association of Heat and Frost Insulators and Asbestos Workers
IAM	International Association of Machinists and aerospace workers

IAMAT	International Association for Medical Assistance to Travelers
IAMSSP	International Association of Marble, Slate and Stone Polishers
IAP	Independent Aging Program
IAPMO	International Association of Plumbing and Mechanical Officials
IAPP	International Association of Pacemaker Patients
IARU	International Amateur Radio Union
IAS	Indicated Air Speed International Association of Siderographers
IASA	Insurance Accounting and Statistical Association
IAT	International Atomic Time
IATA	International Air Transport Association
IATM	International Association of Testing Materials
IATSE	International Alliance of Theatrical Stage Employees
IATV	InterActive TeleVision
IAW	In Accordance With
IBB	International Brotherhood of Boilermakers, iron shipbuilders
IBC	International Brightness Coefficients
IBD	Inflammatory Bowel Disease
IBEC	International Bank for Economic Cooperation
IBEW	International Brotherhood of Electrical Workers
IBFO	International Brotherhood of Firemen and Oilers
IBM	Ion-Beam Machining

IBP	Initial Boiling Point
IBP&AT	International Brotherhood of Painters and Allied Trades
IBPAW	International Brotherhood of Pottery and Allied Workers
IBRD	International Bank for Reconstruction and Development
IBS	International Bible Society
IBT	International Brotherhood of Teamsters, chauffeurs, warehousemen
IBTA	Interest-Bearing Transaction Account
IC	Integrated Circuit Interceptor Command
ICA	International Communication Agency International Communications Association Investment Company Act
ICAO	International Civil Aviation Organization
ICBM	InterContinental Ballistic Missile
ICC	Indian Claims Commission Interstate Commerce Commission
ICCM	InterContinental Cruise Missile
ICCP	Institute for Certification of Computer Professionals
ICE	Initial Cooling Experiment Internal Combustion Engine
ICF	Intermediate Care Facility
ICFTU	International Confederation of Free Trade Unions
ICI	International Commission on Illumination Investment Casting Institute
ICJ	International Court of Justice
ICNI	Integrated Communications-Navigation-Identification

ICP Infection Control Practitioner
IntraCranial Pressure
ICRP International Commission on
Radiological Protection
ICRU International Commission on
Radiological Units and
measures
ICS InterCarrier Sound system
InterCostal Space
ICSH Interstitial-Cell-Stimulating
Hormone
ICSU International Council of
ScientificUnions
ICU Intensive Care Unit
ICW Interrupted Continuous Wave
IntraCoastal Waterway
ICWM International Commission for
Weights and Measures
ICWU International Chemical Workers
Union

ID Idaho
Identification
IDA International Development
Association
IDB Inter-american Development
Bank
IDC Interest During Construction
IDCSP Initial Defense Communications
Satellite Program
IDEC Interior Design Educators
Council
IDP Integrated Data Processing
Intern-architect Development
Program
IDS Image Dissector Scanner
Integrated Data Store
Investigative Dermatological
Society
IDT InterDigital Transducers

IE Immobilized Enzymes
Industrial Engineer

IEA	International Energy Agency
IEC	International Electrotechnical Commission
IEEE	Institute of Electrical and Electronics Engineers
IEES	Induced Electron Emission Spectroscopy
IES	Illuminating Engineering Society
	Inverted Echo Sounder
I&EW	Intelligence and Electronic Warfare
IF	Interferon
	Intermediate Frequency
IFAD	International Fund for Agricultural Development
IFBB	International Federation of BodyBuilders
IFC	International Finance Corporation
IFF	Identification Friend or Foe
IFI	Industrial Fasteners Institute
IFIS	International Food Information Service
IFMA	International Foodservice Manufacturers Association
IFO	Identified Flying Object
IFP&TE	International Federation of Professional and Technical Engineers
IFR	Instrument Flight Rules
IFRB	International Frequency Registration Board
ifs	Independent Front Suspension (Auto)
IFT	Institute of Food Technologists
IFTU	International Federation of Trade Unions
IFUW	International Federation of University Women
IGFA	International Game Fish Association

IGFET	Insulated-Gate Field-Effect Transistor
IGOR	Intercept Ground Optical Recorder
IGR	Insect Growth Regulator
IGT	Insulated-Gate Transistor
IGY	International Geophysical Year
IH	Infectious Hepatitis
IHA	Industrial Heating Association
IHD	International Hydrological Decade
IHF	Institute of High Fidelity
IHP	Indicated HorsePower
IHPVA	International Human Powered Vehicle Association
II	Illegal Immigrant
IIA	Information Industry Association
IIHS	Insurance Institute for Highway Safety
III	Insurance Information Institute
IIR	Integrated Instrumentation Radar
IISS	International Institute for Strategic Studies
IJC	International Joint Commission (US-Canada)
IJWU	International Jewelry Workers' Union
IKE	Ion Kinetic Energy
IKES	Ion Kinetic Energy Spectrometry
IL	Illinois
ILA	International Longshoremen's Association
ILGPNWU	International Leather Goods, Plastics and Novelty Workers Union

ILGWU	International Ladies' Garment Workers' Union
ILO	International Labour Organization
ILS	Instrument (Landing) (Low) Approach) System
ILTF	International Lawn Tennis Federation
ILU	International Laborers Union
ILWU	International Longshoremen's and Warehousemen's Union
ILZRO	International Lead Zinc Research Organization
IM	Interceptor Missile Intermodulation Intramural (Sports) Intramuscular
IMC	Institute of Management Consultants Instrument Meteorological Conditions International Music Council
IMCA	International Motor Contest Association
IMCO	Inter-governmental Maritime Consultative Organization International Metered COmmunication
IMD	International MTM Directorate
IMEP	Indicated Mean Effective Pressure
IMF	International Monetary Fund
IMM	International Monetary Market
IMO	International Money Order
IMP	Interface Message Processor Interplanetary Monitoring (Platform) (Probe)
IMS	International Magnetospheric Study
IMSA	International Metallic Silhouette Association

International Motor Sports
Association
IMTS Improved Mobile-Telephone
System
IMU Inertial Measurement Unit
International Molders and allied
workers Union

in Inch
In Indium
IN Indiana
INCH INtegrated CHopper
INDSCAL INdividual Difference SCALing
INFACT INfant Formula ACTion
(Coalition)
INFCE INternational Fuel Cycle
Evaluation
INFIRS INvented-FIle-seaRch System
INFOL INFormation Oriented
Language
INFORM INternational reference
organization in FORensic
Medicine
INM International Nautical Mile
INN International Nonproprietary
Names (Pharmaceutical)
INPOL POLice INformation (Computer)
INQUA INternational association for
QUAternary research
INS Inertial Navigation System
Immigration and Naturalization
Service
Ion-Neutralization Spectroscopy
INSACS INterState Airways
Communications Stations
INTELSAT INternational
TELcommunications
SATellite
INTERPOL INTERnational criminal POLice
organization

IO Image-Orthicon

I/O Input/Output
IOC Integrated Optic Circuitry
Intergovernmental
Oceanographic Commission
International Olympics
Committee
IOCS Input-Output Control System
IOCU International Organization of
Consumers Unions
ioe Inlet Over Exhaust
IOF Independent Order of Foresters
IOL IntraOcular Lens
IOOF Independent Order of Odd
Fellows
IOP IntraOcular Pressure
IOU I Owe You

IP Impact Point
Innings Pitched
IPA International Platform
Association
IPC Institute for Paper Chemistry
Institute of Printed Circuits
Isopropyl-n-PhenylCarbamate
IPCEA Insulated Power Cable
Engineers Association
IPI Income and Price Index
Inflation Protected Income
IPK International Prototype
Kilogram
IPL Information Processing
Language
Initial Program Loading
IPM Inches Per Minute
Integrated Pest Management
Integrated Program Material
International Prototype Meter
Interruptions Per Minute
IPMS International Polar Motion
Service
IPN Isopropylnitrate
IPOD International Phase of Ocean
Drilling

IPPDSEU International Plate Printers',
Die Stampers' and Engravers'
Union
ipr Inches Per Revolution
IPS Institute of Polar Studies
IPTS International Practical
Temperature Scale

IQ Intelligence Quotient
IQB Individual Quick Blanching
IQF Individually Quick Frozen
IQI Image-Quality Indicators
IQSY International Quiet Sun Year

Ir Iridium
IR Information Retrieval
Infrared
Internal Resistance
I&R Instrumentation and Range
IRA Individual Retirement Account
Intercollegiate Rowing
Association
Irish Republican Army
IRAC Interagency Radio Advisory
Committee
IRBM Intermediate Range Ballistic
Missile
IRC Internal Revenue Code
IRCS Intercomplex Radio
Communications System
IRE Institute of Radio Engineers
IRFNA Inhibited Red Fuming Nitric
Acid
IRIA InfraRed Information and
Analysis
IRIS Information Resources
Information System
IRL Information-Retrieval
Language
IRMI Indirect Reading Measuring
Instruments
IRO International Refugee
Organization

IRR Individual Ready Reserve
Internal Rate of Return
IRRI International Rice Research
Institute
IRRS InfraRed Reflection
Spectroscopy
irs Independent Rear Suspension
IRS Internal Revenue Service
IRSU International Radio Scientific
Union
IRTM InfraRed Thermal Mapper
IRU International Road transport
Union

ISA Instrument Society of America
Intermountain Ski Association
International federation of
national Standardizing
Associations
ISADS Innovative Strategic Aircraft
Design Studies
ISB Independent SideBand
ISBN International Standard Book
Number
ISC International Sportsmen's Club
ISCC Inter-Society Color Council
ISCI Industry Standard Commercial
Identification
ISEE International Sun-Earth
Explorer
ISES International Solar Energy
Society
ISF International Swimming
Federation
ISG Immune Serum Globulin
ISI Institute for Scientific
Information
ISKON International Society for
Krishna cONsciousness
ISM Industrial, Scientific or Medical
ISO International Standard
Organization
ISP Index of Social Position
ISR Intersecting Storage Rings

ISRA	International Ski Racers Association
IST	Insulin Shock Therapy
ISU	International System of Units
ISV	International Scientific Vocabulary
ISX	water-Insoluble Starch Xanthate
IT	Inverse Time
ITA	Independent Truckers Association
	Initial Teaching Alphabet
	International Thermographers Association
ITACS	Integrated Tactical Air Control System
ITB	Integrated Tug-Barge
ITC	Inclusive Tour Charter
	International Tin Council
	International Trade Commission
	InterTropical Convergence
	Investment Tax Credit
ITD	Initial Temperature Difference
ITE	Institute of Transportation Engineers
ITO	International Trade Organization
ITOFCA	Industrial Trailer On Flat Car Association
ITP	Idiopathic Thrombocytopenic Purpuna
ITS	Intermarket Trading System
ITT	Insulin Tolerance Test
ITU	International Telecommunications Union
	International Typographical Union
ITV	Instructional TeleVision
IU	International Unit
IUD	IntraUterine Device
IUE	International Ultraviolet Explorer

International Union of
Electrical, radio and machine
workers

IUEC International Union of Elevator
Constructors

IUGG International Union for Geodesy
and Geophysics

IUJH International Union of
Journeymen Horseshoers

IUMSWA Industrial Union of Marine and
Shipbuilding Workers of
America

IUOE International Union of
Operating Engineers

IUPAC International Union of Pure and
Applied Chemistry

IUPAP International Union of Pure and
Applied Physics

IV IntraVenous

IVA International Volleyball
Association

IVAC In-Vehicular Assistance
Communications

IVF In-Vitro Fertilization

IVM Initial Virtual Memory
(Computer)

IVT IntraVenous Transfusion

IW Isotopic Weight

IWA International Woodworkers of
America

IWC International Whaling
Commission

IWFNA Inhibited White Fuming Nitric
Acid

IWIU Insurance Workers
International Union

IWW Industrial Workers of the World

IYC International Year of the Child

IYRU International Yacht Racing
Union

J

J Joule
JA Junior Achievement
JAMA Journal of the American Medical Association
JAN Joint Army-Navy
JANAF Joint Army-Navy-Air Force
JANGO Junior Army-Navy Guild Organization
JANUS Joint Analog Numerical Understanding System
JATO Jet-Assisted TakeOff

JB Jerusalem Bible
Junction Box
JBHCIU Journeymen Barbers, Hairdressers, Cosmetologists and proprietors International Union

JC Junior Chamber of Commerce or Jaycee
Junior College
JCA Job Corps Administration
JCAE Joint Committee on Atomic Energy

JCAH	Joint Commission on Accreditation of Hospitals
JCL	Job Control Language
JCS	Joint Chiefs of Staff
JDL	Jewish Defense League
JE	Job Enrichment
JEDEC	Joint Electron Device Engineering Council
JETDS	Joint Electronics Type Designation System
JETEC	Joint Electron Tube Engineering Council
JETRO	Japan External TRade Organization
JETS	Junior Engineering Technical Society
JFK	John Fitzgerald Kennedy
JFMIP	Joint Financial Management Improvement Program
JG	Junior Grade
JIC	Joint Industry Conference
JILA	Joint Institute for Laboratory Astrophysics
JIT	Job Instruction Training
JL	Junior League
JND	Just Noticeable Difference
JO	Job Order
JOBS	Job Opportunities in the Business Sector
JOIDES	Joint Oceanographic Institutions for Deep Earth Sampling
JOT	JOb methods Training
JP	Justice of the Peace

J&P   Jackson and Perkins (Roses)
JPL   Jet Propulsion Laboratory

Jr   Junior
JRT   Job-Relations Training

JTU   Jackson Turbidity Unit

JUG   Joint Users Group (Computer)
JUMPS   Joint Uniform Military Pay
    System
JURIS   JUstice Retrieval and Inquiry
    System

JV   Joint Venture
JW   Jehovah's Witnesses

k Kilo
K Kelvin
Potassium
kA Kiloampere
KAB Keep America Beautiful
KANU Kenya African National Union
KAO Kuiper Airborne Observatory
KAT Key to Address Transformation

kb Kilobar
KB Kelly Bushing (Drilling)

kc Kilocycle
KC Kansas City
kcal Kilocalorie
KCB Knight Commander of the Bath
KCBOT Kansas City Board Of Trade
kCi Kilocurie
KCIA Korean Central Intelligence
Agency
kc/s KiloCycles per Second

KD Knocked Down (Cartons and
Furnishings)
KDP Potassium Dihydrogen
Phosphate

KE	Kinetic Energy
KeV	Kilo Electron Volt
KEWB	Kinetic Experiment Water Boiler
kg	Keg
	Kilogram mass
kG	Kilogauss
KG	Knight of the Garter
KGB	Komitet Gosudarstvennoye Bezopastnosti (Russian Security Police)
kgf	KiloGram Force
KGPS	KiloGrams Per Second
kHz	KiloHertz
KIA	Killed In Action
KJ	Knee Jerk
KJV	King James Version (Bible)
KK	Knee Kick
KKK	Ku Klux Klan
kl	Kiloliter
km	Kilometer
kM	Kilomega
KMPS	KiloMeters Per Second
KMT	Kuomintang (Taiwan)
kN	Kilonewton
KNUFNS	Kampuchean National United Front for National Salvation (Cambodia)
KO	Knock Out
KofC	Knights of Columbus
KofL	Knights of Labor
KOA	Kampgrounds Of America
KOC	Cathodal Opening Contraction
KOH	Potassium HydroOxide

KP	Key Punch
	Kings Pawn (Chess)
	Kitchen Police
	Knights of Pythias
	Kodak Process resist
kPa	Kilopascal
Kpc	Kiloparsec
kph	Kilometers Per Hour

Kr	Krypton
KS	Kansas
ksi	Kinetic pounds per Square Inch
KSR	Keyboard Send and Receive
kt	Kiloton
	Knot
KUB	Kidney, Ureter, Bladder
KUT	Potassium, Uranium and Thorium
kV	KiloVolt
kVA	KiloVolt-Ampere
KVAR	Kilovar
kVp	KiloVolts, Peak
kW	KiloWatt
KW	Kenilworth (Truck)
KWHR	KiloWatt HouR
KWIC	Key Word In Context
KWOC	Key Word Out of Context
KY	Kentucky

l Liter
L Large
Length
Roman Numeral 50
La Lanthanum
LA Least Action
Los Angeles
Louisiana
LAC Lunar Aeronautical Chart
LACE Liquid Air Cycle Engine
LACIE Large Area Crop Inventory
Experiment
LADAR LAser raDAR
LADD Low Angle Drogued Delivery
LAER Lowest Achievable Emission
Rate
LAFTA Latin America Free Trade
Association
LAGEOS LAser GEOdynamic Satellite
LAMPS Light Airborne Multi-Purpose
System
LANBY Large Automatic Navigation
BuoY
LAP Leucine AminoPeptidase
LAS Laboratory of Atmospheric
Sciences

Linear Alkyl Sulfonates
LASA Large Aperture Seismic Array
LASCR Light-Activated Silicon Control
Rectifier
LASER Light Amplification by
Stimulated Emission of
Radiation
LASH Lighter Aboard SHip
LASL Los Alamos Scientific
Laboratory
LATS Limited Access Telephone
Service
LAW League of American Wheelmen

lb Pound mass
LB Light Bomber
Linebacker
Local Battery
LBC Loose Bladder Construction
(Ball)
lbf Pound force
LBJ Lyndon Baines Johnson
LBM Laser-Beam Machining
Low Band Monochrome
LBP Length Between Perpendiculars
Personnel Landing Boat
LBV Vehicle Landing Boat

lc Lower Case
LC Landing Craft
Letter of Credit
Library of Congress
Line Circuit
Liquid Chromatography
LCA Lutheran Church in America
LCB Longitudinal Center of
Buoyancy
LCC Life-Cycle Costing
Low-Current Configuration
LCD Least Common Denominator
Light-Crystal Diode
Liquid Crystal Display
LCDS Low Cost Development System

LCI	Landing Craft Infantry
LCM	Landing Craft (Mechanized) (Mobile)
	Large Core Memory
	Least Common Multiple
LCMS	Lutheran Church-Missouri Synod
LCN	Load Classification Number
LCP	Landing Craft Personnel
LCS	Landing Craft Support
	Large Core Storage
LCT	Landing Craft Tank
LCWE	Lausanne Committee for World Evangelism
LD	Lethal Dosage
	Linnz-Donnewitz (Steel Process)
L/D	Lift divided by Drag
LDCs	Less Developed Countries
L&DCIU	Laundry and Dry Cleaning International Union
LDL	Low-Density Lipoproteins
LDMS	Laboratory Data Management System
LDR	Light-Dependent Resistor
LDS	Latter-Day Saints (Mormon)
	Local Distributing Service (TV Cable)
LDV	Laser Doppler Velocimeter
LE	Lupus Erythematosus
LEA	Local Education Agency
LEAA	Law Enforcement Assistance Administration
LECA	Lightweight Expanded Clay Aggregate
LED	Light Emitting Diode
LEED	Low-Energy-Electron Diffraction
LEEP	Law Enforcement Education Program
LEGIS	LEGislative Information and Status system

LEIN Law Enforcement InformationNetwork
LEIU Law Enforcement Intelligence Unit
LEM Lunar Excursion Module
LEP Large Electron-Proton
LERA Limited Employee Retirement Account
LESS Least cost EStimating and Scheduling
LET Linear Energy Transfer
LEV Lunar Excursion Vehicle

LF Loan Forgiveness
Lost on Foul
Low Flange
Low Frequency
LFA Lime Fly Ash (Aggregate)
LFD Least Fatal Dose
LFSE Ligand Field Stabilization Energy
LFT Linear FooT

L/G Liquid-to-Gas

LH Left Hand
Lutenizing Hormone
LHA Local Hour Angle
LHD *Litteris Humanioribus Doctor* (Doctor of Humanities)
Load-Haul-Dump
LHV Low Heat Value

li Link
Li Lithium
LI Limit of Identification
Long Island
LIBEC LIght BEhind Camera
LIFO Last In, First Out
LIFT Logically Integrated FORTRAN Translator
LIL Large Ion Lithophile

LIM	Linear Induction Motor
LINACS	LINear ACceleratorS
LIS	Lithium diIodoSalicylate
LITE	Legal Information Through Electronics
LKS	Liver, Kidneys and Spleen
LL	Line Link
	Little League
LLB	Left LineBacker (Football)
	Legum Baccalaureus (Bachelor of Laws)
LLC	Liquid-Liquid Chromatography
LLSIL	Lower Living Standard Income Level
lm	Lumen
LM	Lunar Module
LMC	Large Magellanic Cloud
LMFBR	Liquid Metal-cooled Fast-Breeder Reactor
LMFR	Liquid-Metal Fuel Reactor
LMG	Light Machine Gun
LMSA	Labor-Management Services Administration
LMT	Local Mean Time
LNBC	Laymen's National Bible Committee
LNG	Liquefied Natural Gas
LO	Liaison Officer (Military)
LOB	Line Of Balance
LOCA	Loss-Of-Coolant Accident (Reactor)
LOD	Line Of Duty
LOFT	Loss of Fluid Test
LOGANDS	LOGical commANDS
LOGRAM	LOGical progRAM
LOLP	Loss Of Load Probability
LOOM	Loyal Order Of Moose

LOPO	LOw-POwer water boiler reactor
LOR	Low-frequency OmniRange
	Lunar Orbit Rendezvous
LORAN	LOng-RAnge Navigation
LOS	Line Of Scrimmage
	Line Of Sight
	Loss Of Signal
LOWV	League Of Women Voters
LOX	Liquid OXygen
LOZ	Liquid OZone
LP	Limiting Proportions
	Linear Programming
	Long Playing
LPE	Liquid-Phase Epitaxy
lpf	Low-Power Field
LPG	Liquefied Petroleum Gas
	Liquid Propane Gas
LPGA	Ladies Professional Golfers Association
LPM	Lines Per Minute
LPN	Licensed Practical Nurse
LPOF	Low-Pressure Oil-Filled (Cable)
LPOOC	Lake Placid Olympic Organizing Committee
LPS	Low-Pressure Sodium (Traffic Light)
LPSA	Lithographic Preparatory Services Association
Lr	Lawrencium
LR	Labeled Release
	Load-Resistor
	Long Rifle
LRTP	Long-Running Thermal Precipitation
LRU	Least Recently Used
LRV	Light Rail Vehicle
	Lunar Roving Vehicle
LS	Landing Ship
	Left Safety (Football)
	Log-Skidder (Tires)

LSAT	Law School Admissions Test
LSB	Least Significant Bit
LSC	Laser-Supported Combustion
LSD	Landing Ship Dock
	LySergic acid Diethylamide
LSG	Low-Stress Grinding
LSI	Large Scale Integration
LSM	Letter Sorting Machine
LSMR	Landing Ship Medium, Rocket
LSS	Loop Switching System
LST	Landing Ship Tank
	Large Space Telescope
LSV	Lunar Surface Vehicle
LT	Left Tackle
	Low Tension
LTC	Load Tap-Charger (Transformer)
LTD	Long Term Debt
LTS	Launch Tracking System (Space)
LTTMT	Low-Temperature ThermoMechanical Treatment (Steel)
Lu	Lutetium
LU	Logic Unit
LUF	Lowest Usable Frequency
LUHF	Lowest Useful High Frequency
LULAC	League of United Latin American Citizens
LUTOM	Land Use Trade Off Model
LUV	Light Utility Vehicle
LV	Left Ventricle
	Light Value (Photography)
LVDT	Linear-Variable-Differential Transformer
LVN	Licensed Vocational Nurse
LVT	Landing Vehicle, Tracked
LVW	Linked Vertical Well (Coal Gasification)

LWA Limited-Work Authorization
lwb Long WheelBase
LWF Luminous Wall Firing
LWK Live Weight Kill
LWL Length on load WaterLine
LWR Light Water Reactor

158

lx Lux

LZ Landing Zone

m Meter
M Magazine (Rifle)
Mass
Medium
Mega
Roman Numeral 1,000
mA MilliAmpere
MA *Magister Artium* (Master of
Arts)
Manpower Administration
Maritime Administration
Massachusetts
Mechanical Advantage
MegAmpere
MAA Mathematics Association of
America
MethaneArsonic Acid
(Herbicide)
MAAG Military Assistance Advisory
Group
MAC Maximum Allowable
Concentration
Mean Aerodynamic Chord
Military Airlift Command
MACAP Major Appliance Consumer
Action Panel

MAD	Magnetic Anomaly Detector
	Mean Absolute Deviation
	Mosquito Abatement District
MAE	Master of Arts in Education
maf	Moisture and Air Free
MAF	Marine Amphibious Force
MAGLEV	MAGnetic LEVitation (Mass Transit)
MAGS	Mexican American Graduate Studies
MAH	Magnesium Aluminate Hydrate
MAI	Mean Annual Increment (Tree Growth)
	Member American Institute (Appraisers)
MALD	Master of Arts in Law and Diplomacy
MALS	Master of Arts in (Liberal Studies) (Library Science)
MANIAC	Mathematical Analyser Numerical Indicator And Computer
MANMAN	MANufacturing MANagement
MAO	MonoAmine Oxidase
MAP	Macro Assembly Program
	Middle Atmosphere Program
	Military Assistance Program
	Modified American Plan (Travel)
	Multiple Aim Point
MAPI	Machinery and Allied Products Institute
MAR	Master of Arts in Religion
	Memory Address Register
MARC	Mining And Reclamation Council
MARR	Minimum Attractive Rate of Return
MARS	Military Amateur Radio Service
MAS	Magnesium AluminiSilicate
	Management Advisory Services
MASH	Mobile Army Surgical Hospital
MAST	Military Assistance to Safety and Traffic

MAT Master of Arts in Teaching
Micro Alloy Transistor
MATC MAximum Toxicant
Concentration
MATS Military Air Transport Service
MATV Master-Antenna TeleVision
MAW Machinists and Aerospace
Workers

mb Millibar
MB *Medicinae Baccalaureus*
(Bachelor of Medicine)
Medium Bomber
MBA Marching Bands of America
Master of Business
Administration
Mortgage Bankers Association
Motorized Bicycle Association
MBALE 1,000 Bales
MBBL 1,000 Barrels
MBE Member of the British Empire
Molecular Beam Epitaxy
MBF Moving-Bed Filter (Waste)
MBFR Mutual Balanced Force
Reduction
MBN Mutual Black Network
MBO Management By Objectives
MBPS Million Bits Per Second
MBS MegaBits per Second
Mutual Broadcasting System,
Inc.
MBU 1,000 Bushels
MBX Management By eXception

mc Megacycle
MC Master of Ceremonies
Medium Curing (Cement)
Memory Controller
Metal Case (Bullet)
Metal Clad (Wire)
Mortgage Constant
MCA Manufacturing Chemists
Association

Multiprocessor Communications Adapter

Music Critics Association

MCAR 1,000 Carats

MCAT Medical College Admissions Test

MCBR Master Car Builders' Rules

MCC Mechanical-Chemical Code

Minimum Circumscribed Circle (Screws)

Motor Cycling Club

MCD Mean Cell Diameter

MCE Master of Christian Education

Master of Civil Engineering

MCF Military Computer Family

1,000 Cubic Feet

mcg Microgram

MCH Mean Corpuscular Hemoglobin

MCI Meal Combat Individual (Ration)

MCJ Master of Comparative Jurisprudence

MCL Master of Civil Law

Maximum Contaminant Level

Mid Clavicular Line

MCLOF Market Center Limit Order File (Stock)

MCN Museum Computer Network

MCP Master Control Program

Master of City Planning

MCRB Motor Carrier Rate Bureau

MCRT Mean Cell Residence Time

MCS Management Control System

Master of Computer Science

Mine Countermeasures Support (Ship)

Modular Component System

MCT Mean Circulation Time

MCU Machine Control Unit

MCUG Military Computer Users Group

MCV Mean Corpuscular Volume

MCW Modulated Continuous Wave

Md Mendelevium

MD	Magnetic Deflection
	Maryland
	Muscular Dystrophy
	Doctor of Medicine
MDA	Minimum Descent Altitude
MDAR	Minimum Daily Adult Requirement
MDF	Main Distributing Frame (Furnace)
MDI	Market Development Index
MDM	Mechanically Deboned Meat
MDMV	Maize Dwarf Mosaic Virus
MDO	Medium Density Overlag (Plywood)
	Monthly Debit Ordinary
MDR	Minimum Daily Requirement
mds	Millidarcies
MDS	Malfunction Detection System
	Meteoroid Detection Satellite
	Microcomputer Development Systems
MDT	Mountain Daylight Time
MDTA	Manpower Development and Training Act
MDTS	Multiple Dealer Trading System (Stock)
MDW	Military District of Washington
ME	Magnetic Electric
	Maine
	Master Element
	Master of Engineering
	Mechanical Engineer
	Methodist Episcopal
'	Middle East
	Muzzle Energy (Bullet)
MEA	Minimum En route Altitude
MEB	Marine Expeditionary Brigade
MEBA	Marine Engineers Beneficial Association
MECI	Manufacturing Engineering Certification Institute
MED	Minimal Erythemal Dose

MEES	Middle East Economic Survey
MEF	Marine Expeditionary Force
MEK	Methyl-Ethyl-Ketone
MEMA	Motor and Equipment Manufacturers Association
MEP	Master of Engineering Physics
MEPSP	Miniature Excitatory Post Synaptic Potentials (Ear)
mEq	Milliequivalent
MES	Marketable Equity Securities
MESA	Mechanics Educational Society of America
	Mining Enforcement and Safety Administration
MESBIC	Minority Enterprise Small Business Investment Companies
METO	Maximum Except for Takeoff (Air)
	Middle East Treaty Organization
MeV	Million Electron Volts
MEW	Microwave Early Warning
mf	Microfrar
MF	Machine-Finished (Paper)
	Magnetic Focus
	Master of Forestry
	Medium Frequency
	Multi-Filamentary
MFA	Master of Fine Arts
	Men's Fashion Association
mfd	Microfarad
MFD	Magnetofluiddynamics
MFH	Master of FoxHounds
MFM	Magneto Fluid Mechanic
MFN	Most Favored Nation
MFOA	Municipal Finance Officers Association
MFP	Mean Free Path
MFS	Master of Food Science
MFSS	Missile Flight Safety System
MFT	Mean Free Time
	Motor Freight Terminal

MFTL Milli-FooT-Lamberts

mg Milligram
Mg Magnesium
  Megagram
MG Machine-Glazed (Paper)
  Machine Gun
  Morris Garages (Auto)
  Motor Generator
  Myasthenia Gravis
MGC Mean Geometric Chord
mgd Million Gallons per Day
MGD MagnetoGas Dynamics
MGIC Mortgage Guaranty Insurance
  Corporation (Maggie Mae)
MG&L Measurement of Gains and
  Losses
MGM Mentally Gifted Minors
MgO MaGnesium Oxide
MGT Metal-Gate Transistor

mH MilliHenry
MH Master of Hounds
MHA Master in Hospital
  Administration
MHC Mine Hunter, Coastal
MHCP Mean Horizontal CandlePower
MHD Magneto-HydroDynamics
  Mail Handlers Division
MHE Master of Home Economics
MHI Manufactured Housing
  Institute
  Material Handling Institute
MHL Master of Hebrew Literature
MHR Maximum-attainable Heart
  Rate
MHW Mean High Water
MHX Material Handling eXpense
MHz MegaHertz

mi Mile
MI Malleable Iron
  Marginal Income
  Michigan

Microbiological Inputs
  (Canning)
Military Intelligence
MIA Master of International Affairs
Missing In Action
MIB Medical Information Bank
MIBK Methyl IsoButyl Ketone
MIC Maximum Inscribed Circle
  (Screws)
Monolithic Integrated Circuit
Motorcycle Industry Council
MICR Magnetic Ink Character
  Recognition
MICU Mobile Intensive Care Unit
MID Master of Industrial Design
Meat Inspection Division
MIDAS MIssile Defense Alarm System
MIE Master of Irrigation
  Engineering
MIG Metal Inert Gas (Welding)
MIkhail Gurevich (Plane)
MIKES Mass-analyzed Ion Kinetic
  Energy Spectrometry
MIL 1,000,000
MILPERCEN MILitary PERsonnel CENter
MILR Master of Industrial and Labor
  Relations
MIL-SPECS MILitary SPECificationS
MILSTAMP MILitary Standard
  Transportation And
  Movement Procedures
MIL-STD MILitary STanDards
MIMR Magnetic Ink Mark Recognition
MIN Marine Identification Number
MIP Monthly Investment Plan
MIRAN MIssile RANging
MIRV Multiple Independently
  targeted Re-entry Vehicle
MIS Management Information
  System
Master of International Service
Metal-Insulator (Semi-
  conductor) (Silicon)

MIST Medical Information Service via Telephone

MJ Master of Journalism
Megajoule

MK Morse Key
mks Meter-Kilogram-Second
MKSA Meter-Kilogram-Second-Ampere

ml Milliliter
mL MilliLambert
ML Mining and Logging (Tires)
Muzzleloader
MLA Master of Landscape Architecture
Modern Language Association
MLB MultiLayer Board
1,000 Pounds
MLBPA Major League Baseball Players Association
MLC Mixed Leukocyte Culture
MultiLayer Ceramic (Capacitor)
MLD (Medium) (Minimum) Lethal Dose
MLF MultiLateral Force
MLLP Manned Lunar Landing Program
MLR Mined Land Reclamation
MLRC Multi-Level Rail Car
MLS Master of Library Science
Microwave Landing System
MLSS Mixed Liquor Suspended Solids
MLT Mass, Length, Time
MLTN 1,000 Long ToNs
MLUA Major League Umpires Association
MLVSS Mixed Liquor Volatile Suspended Solids
MLW Mean Low Water

mm Millimeter
mM Millimole

MM	Magnetic-Mechanical
	Master of Music
	Metronome
	Million
	Mucous Membrane
	Multipolar Magnetic (Sun)
MMA	Merchant Marine Academy
	Metropolitan Museum of Art
MMCs	Money Market Certificates
MMD	Mass Median Diameter
MME	Master of (Music Education) (Mechanical Engineering)
MMF	MagnetoMotive Force
MMFPA	Man-Made Fiber Producers Association
MMH	MonoMethyl Hydrazine
mmm	Micromillimeter
MMPA	Marine Mammals Protection Act
MMR	Measles, Mumps, Rubella
MMRBM	Mobile Mid-Range Ballistic Missile
MMT	Materials and Manufacturing Technology
	Methyleyclopentadienyl Manganese Tricarbonyl
	Million Metric Tons
	Multiple-Mirror Telescope
MMTN	Manned Mission Tracking Net
Mn	Manganese
MN	Magnetic North
	Minnesota
MNA	Master of Nursing Administration
MNC	MultiNational Company
MNE	Master of Nuclear Engineering
MNOS	Metal-Nitride-Oxide-Silicon
MNP	Medical Nurse Practitioner
MNR	National Revolutionary Movement (Bolivia)
	Minimum Noise Routing
MNS	Master of Nutritional Science

Mo	Molybdenum
MO	Mail Order
	Manufacturing Order
	Medical Officer
	Method of Operation
	Missouri
	Money Order
MOA	Metropolitan Opera Association
MODS	Manned Orbital Development Station
MOE	Measure Of Effectiveness
MOIG	Master of Occupational Information and Guidance
moiv	Mechanically Operated Inlet Valve
mol	Mole
MOL	Manned Orbiting Laboratory
MOMA	Museum Of Modern Art
MON	Motor Octane Number
MONEX	MONsoon EXperiment
MOPA	Master Oscillator Power Amplifier
MOPED	MOtor-assisted PEDal cycle
MOR	Middle Of the Road
MORGA	Municipal ORGanization Act
MOS	Metal Oxide Semiconductor
MOSFET	MOS Field-Effect Transistor
MOST	MOS Transistor
MOUSE	Minimum Orbital Unmanned Satellite, Earth
MOVE	Multiple Occupancy VEhicles
MOWW	Military Order of World Wars
MOY	Man Of the Year
mp	Melting Point
MP	Main Program (Computer)
	Maritime Polar (Air Mass)
	Match Pointer
	Member of Parliament (British)
	Military Police
	Modus Ponens (Logic)
MPA	Magazine Publishers Association

Master of (Professional Accounting) (Public Affairs)

MPAA Motion Picture Association of America

MPBPAW Metal Polishers, Buffers, Platers and Allied Workers

Mpc Megaparsec

MPC Maximum Possible Concentration

Medium Processing Channel (Carbon)

Military Payment Certificate

MPD Magnetoplasmadynamics

Maximum Permissible Dose

MPE Master of Physical Education

MPEAA Motion Picture Export Association of America

MPFG 1,000 ProoF Gallons

mpg Miles Per Gallon

mph Miles Per Hour

MPH Master of Public Health

MPI Mean Point of Impact

MPIF Metal Powder Industries Federation

MPL Master of Patent Law

Maximum Permissible Level

Motivated Productivity Level

MPMO Motion Picture Machine Operators

MPN Most Probable Number

MPS Master of Personnel Service

Meters Per Second

Minimum Property Standards

MP(S)P Mechanically Processed (Species) Product

MPU Microcomputer

MPX Multiplex

MQ Metol-hydroQuinone (Photography)

mr (Millirad) (Millirem) (Milliroentgen)

MR Market Research
Master Relay (Electrical)
Memory Reclaimer (Computer)
Mentally Retarded
Mill Run
Missionary Rector
Mixture Ratio

MRA Maximum Reresponse Axis
MRAC Meter Reading Access Circuit
MRC Medical Reserve Corps
MRCA Multi-Role Combat Aircraft
MRE Master of Religious Education
Meal, Ready-to-Eat
MRL Maximum Record Level
Medical Record Librarian
MRN Meteorological Rocket Network
MRO Maintenance, Repair and
Operating
MRP Magnum Rifle Powder
Master of Regional Planning
Material Requirements
Planning
Midland Racing Partnership
MRS Medium-Range Surveillance

ms Millisecond
MS Machine Steel
Magnetic-Selsyn
Manuscript
Master Switch
Military Standards
Mississippi
Motor Ship
Multiple Sclerosis
M&S Marshall and Swift cost index
MSA Marigold Society of America
Master of Science in Agriculture
Mine Safety Appliances
Mycological Society of America
MSAE Master of Science in
Aeronautical Engineering
MSAM Master of Science in Applied
Mathematics

MSAWS	Minimum Safe Altitude Warning System
MSB	Most Significant Bit
MSBA	Master of Science in Business Administration
MSBC	Master of Science in Building Construction
MSC	Manned Spacecraft Center
	Medical Service Corps
MSCP	Mean Spherical CandlePower
MSCS	Master of Science in Computer Science
MSE	Master of Science in (Education) (Engineering)
	Mean Square Error
MSEE	Master of Science in Electrical Engineering
MSEM	Master of Science in Engineering (Mechanics) (of Mines)
MSF	Master of Science in Forestry
	Motorcycle Safety Foundation
	1,000 Square Feet
MSG	MonoSodium Glutamate
MSH	Melanocyte-Stimulating Hormone
MSHA	Mine Safety and Health Administration
MSI	Medium Scale Integration
MSJ	Master of Science in Journalism
MSL	Master of Science in Linguistics
	Mean Sea Level
MSM	Master of Sacred Music
MSME	Master of Science in Mechanical Engineering
MSO	Mine Sweeping Ocean (Ship)
MSOs	Multiple-System Operators
MSP	Measurement Sensitive Products
	Microsuspension Seeded Polymerization
MSPA	Motor Sports Press Association
MSPB	Merit Systems Protection Board

MSPE	Master of Science in Physical Education
MSPH	Master of Science in Public Health
MSR	Main Supply Route (Military)
	Missile Site Radar
MSRA	Mini Stock Racing Association
MSRTS	Migrant Student Record Transfer System
MSS	Manufacturers Standardization Society
	Master of Social Service
	Measurement Standard
	Sensitivity
MSSE	Master of Science in Sanitary Engineering
MST	Master of Science in Teaching
	Mountain Standard Time
MSTN	1,000 Short ToNs
MSTS	Military Sea Transportation Service
MSW	Master of Social Work
mt	Megaton
MT	Maritime Tropical (Air Mass)
	Metric Ton
	Montana
MTA	Motion Time Analysis
MTBF	Mean Time Between Failures
MTBSF	Mean Time Between Service Failures
MTC	Master Training Concept
	Multistate Tax (Commission) (Compact)
MTD	Mean Temperature Difference
MTF	Mechanical Time Fuse
	Modulation Transfer Function
MTI	Moving-Target Indicator
MTM	Method-Times Measurement (C-Clerical, V-Machine Tools, M-Magnification)
MTMC	Military Traffic Management Command

MTN	Multilateral Trade Negotiations
MTNA	Music Teachers National Association
MTO	Mediterranean Theater of Operations
MTOCs	MicroTubule-Organizing Centers
MTOS	Metal-Thick-Oxide Semiconductor
MTP	Multiply Twinned Particles
MTS	Machine Tractor Station
	Motion Time Standards
MTSS	Military Test Space Station
MTTR	Mean Time To Repair
MTU	Magnetic Tape Unit
	Multiplexer and Terminal Unit
MU	Machine Unit
MUF	Maximum Usable Frequency
MUG	Maximum Usable Gain
MULE	Modular Universal Laser Equipment
MUN	Million UNits
MUP	Master of Urban Planning
MUPO	Maximum Undisturbed Power Output
mV	Millivolt
MV	Mixture Velocity (Auto Fuel)
mVA	Million Volt-Ampere
MVM	Minimum Virtual Memory
MVMA	Motor Vehicle Manufacturers Association
MVP	Most Valuable Player
MVS	Multiple Virtual Storages
mw	Molecular Weight
mW	Milliwatt
MW	MegaWatt
M/W	Minorities and Women
MWA	Modern Woodmen of America
MWd	MegaWatt-Days
MWD	Measurement While Drilling (Oil)

Molecular Weight Distribution
MWe MegaWatt Electric
MWG Music Wire Gage
MWP Maximum Working Pressure
MWV Maximum Working Voltage

Mx Maxwell
MX Mobile Missle eXperimental

MYOB Mind Your Own Business

N Newton (Unit of Force)
Nitrogen
North
Na Sodium
NA National Association (Banking)
North America
Not Available
Numerical Aperture
Nurses Aide
N/A Not Applicable
NAA NaphthaleneAcetic Acid
National Aeronautic Association
National Archery Association
National Association of
Accountants
Neutron Activation Analysis
NAACP National Association for the
Advancement of Colored
People
NAAD National Association of
Aluminum Distributors
NAAO National Association of
Amateur Oarsmen
NAARS National Automated Accounting
Research System

NAB National Alliance of
Businessmen
National Association of
Broadcasters
NABBA National Amateur
BodyBuilding Association
NABET National Association of
Broadcast Employees and
Technicians
NABT National Association of Biology
Teachers
NABUG National Association of
Broadcast Unions and Guilds
NABW National Association of Bank
Women
NAC National Association of
Composers
NACC National Automobile Chamber
of Commerce
NACE National Association of
Corrosion Engineers
NACIS NAtional Credit and
Information Service
NACM National Association of Credit
Management
NACo National Association of
COunties
NACOM NAtional COMmunications
system
NACP National Association of Colored
People
NACU National Association of Colleges
and Universities
NAD National Academy of Design
NADA National Automobile Dealers
Association
NADP Nicotinamide-Adenine
Dinucleotide Phosphate
NADS National Association of Drag
Strips
NAE National Academy of
Engineering
National Association of
Evangelicals

NAEB National Association of
Educational Broadcasters

NAED National Association of
Electrical Distributors

NAFB National Association of Farm
Broadcasters

NAFEM National Association of Food
Equipment Manufacturers

NAHB National Association of Home
Builders

NAHF National Association of Home
Furnishers

NAIA National Association of
Intercollegiate Athletics

NAIC National Association of
Insurance Commissioners
National Association of
Investment Clubs

NAIFA National Association of
Independent Fee Appraisers

NAIFR National Association of
Independent Food Retailers

NAIRS National Athletic Injury
Reporting System

NAJE National Association of Jazz
Educators

NAL National Agricultural Library

NALC National Association of Letter
Carriers

NALPM National Association of
Lithographic Plate
Manufacturers

NALS National Association of Legal
Secretaries

NALSA North American Land Sailing
Association

NALU National Association of Life
Underwriters

NAM National Association of
Manufacturers
NonAdditive Mixing

NAMBO National Association of Motor
Bus Operators

NAMDI	NAtional Marine Data Inventory
NAMF	National Association of Metal Finishers
NAMH	National Association for Mental Health
NAMIA	National Association of Mutual Insurance Agents
NAMM	National Association of Music Merchants
NANA	North American and North Atlantic area
NANWEP	NAvy Numerical WEather Prediction
NAPA	National Automotive Parts Association
NAPCA	National Air Pollution Control Administration
NAPFE	National Alliance of Postal and Federal Employees
NAPM	National Association of Pattern Manufacturers
	National Association of Purchasing Management
NAPS	National Association of Postal Supervisors
NAR	National Association of Realtors
NARCE	National Association of Retired Civil Employees
NARD	National Association for Retail Druggists
NAREB	National Association of Real Estate Boards
NARFE	National Association of Retired Federal Employees
NARGUS	National Association of Retail Grocers of the United States
NARP	National Association of Railroad Passengers
NARS	National Archives and Records Service
NART	North American Racing Team
NARTB	National Association of Radio and Television Broadcasters

NAS   National Academy of Sciences
National Aircraft Standards
National Audubon Society
Naval Air Station
NASA   National Aeronautics and Space
Administration
NASBA   National Association of State
Boards of Accountancy
NASCAR   National Association for Stock
Car Auto Racing
NASD   National Association of Security
Dealers
NASDAQ   National Association of Security
Dealers Automated Quotation
NASDS   National Association of Skin
Diving Schools
NASL   North American Soccer League
NASM   National Association of Schools
of Music
NATAS   National Academy of Television
Arts and Sciences
NATO   No Action, Talk Only
North Atlantic Treaty
Organization
NATRA   National Association of TV and
Radio Artists
NATTS   National Association of Trade
and Technical Schools
NAUI   National Association of
Underwater Instructors
NAUSS   National Association of
Uniformed ServiceS
NAV   Net Asset Value
NAVAIR   NAVal AIR
NAVAR   NAVigation radAR
NAVCAD   NAVal aviation CADet
NAVSHIPS   NAVal SHIPS
NAVWEPS   NAVal WEaPonS
NAW   National Association of
Wholesalers-distributors
NAWA   National Automobile
underWriters' Association
NAWAPA   North American Water And
Power Alliance

NAWAS   NAtional WArning System

Nb   Niobium
NB   National Ballet
NBA   National Basketball Association
National Boxing Association
National Buyers Association
NBC   National Baseball Congress
National Broadcasting
Company, Inc.
National Building Code
NBER   National Bureau of Economic
Research
NBFA   National Business Forms
Association
NBFM   Narrow Band Frequency
Modulation
NBFU   National Board of Fire
Underwriters
NBL   National Basketball League
NBN   National Black Network
NBR   Nitrile Butadiene Rubber
NBS   National Bureau of Standards

NC   National Coarse (Screw
Threads)
North Carolina
Numerically Controlled
Nurses Corps
N/C   No Charge
NCA   National Canners Association
National Carousel Association
National Cattlemen's
Association
National Clearinghouse on
Aging
National Coal Association
National Constructors
Association
National Council on Alcoholism
NeuroCirculatory Asthenia
NCAA   National Collegiate Athletic
Association

NCAC	National Council of Acoustical Consultants
NCAN	National Coalition of American Nuns
NCARB	National Council of Architectural Registration Boards
NCASI	National Council for Air and Stream Improvement
NCATE	National Council for Accreditation of Teacher Education
NCBC	National Conference of Black Churchmen
NCC	National Climactic Center
	National Cotton Council
	National Council of Churches
NCCJ	National Conference of Christians and Jews
NCEE	National Council of Engineering Examiners
NCES	National Center for Educational Statistics
NCF	Net Cash Flow
NCFA	National Collection of Fine Arts
NCGA	National Council on Governmental Accounting
NCHRP	National Cooperative Highway Research Program
NCHS	National Center for Health Statistics
NCI	National Cancer Institute
	National Captioning Institute (Deaf)
NCIAC	National Construction Industry Arbitration Council
NCM	Natural Clay Mosaic
NCNEL	Normalized Community Noise Equivalent Level
NCO	Non-Commissioned Officer
NCOA	National Council On Aging
NCP	Natural Clay Pavers
NCPAC	National Conservative Political Action Committee

NCRP	National Committee on Radiation Protection and measurements
NCS	NonCrystalline Solid
NCSA	National Crushed Stone Association
NCSC	National Center for State Courts
	National Council of Senior Citizens
NCTA	National Cable Television Association
NCTE	National Council of Teachers of English
NCUA	National Credit Union Administration
NCWEC	National Credit Women's Executive Committee
Nd	Neodymium
ND	No Decision
	North Dakota
NDA	New Drug Application
NDB	NonDirectional radio Beacon
NDE	NonDestruction Examination
NDEA	National Defense Education Act
NDELA	N-nitrosodiethanolamine
NDGA	NorDihydroGuaiaretic Acid
NDP	Neighborhood Development Program
NDS	Nuclear Detection Satellite
NDSL	National Direct Student Loan
NDT	Nil-Ductility Transition temperature (Steel)
	Non Destructive Testing
NDU	National Defense University
Ne	Neon
NE	Nebraska
NEA	National Education Association
	National Endowment for the Arts
	Negative-Electron Affinity
	Newspaper Enterprise Association

NEAT	National Electronic Automatic Technique
NEB	New English Bible
NEC	National Electric Code
	Navy Enlisted Code
NECA	National Electrical Contractors Association
NEH	National Endowment for the Humanities
NEIS	National Energy Information System
NEISS	National Electronic Injury Surveillance System
NEL	Navy Electronics Laboratory
NEMA	National Electrical Manufacturer's Association
NEP	National Energy Plan
	New Economic Policy
	Noise Equivalent Power
NEPA	National Environmental Policy Act
NERC	National Electric Reliability Council
NESHAPS	National Emission Standards for Hazardous Air PollutantS
NESS	National Environmental Satellite Service
NET	National Educational Television
NETOPEC	Nations Exporting To OPEC
Nf	Nanofarad
NF	National Fine (Screw Threads)
	National Formulary
	Nitrogen Fluoride
	Normal Frequency
NFA	National Firearms Act
NFAA	National Field Archery Association
NFC	National Football Conference
NFDA	National Funeral Directors Association
NFEWA	Newspaper Food Editors and Writers Association
NFF	National Football Foundation

NFFE National Federation of Federal Employees
NFFS Non-Ferrous Founders' Society
NFIB National Federation of Independent Business
NFL National Football League
NFMA National Forest Management Act
NFMC National Federation of Music Clubs
NFO National Farmers Organization
NFOC Naval Flight Officer Candidate
NFPA National Fire Protection Association (Code)
National Food Processors Association
NFPCA National Fire Prevention and Control Administration
NFS National Forest Service

NG National Guard
NGA National Governor's Association
NGC National Gambling Commission
New General Catalogue (Astronomy)
NGF National Golf Foundation
Nerve Growth Factor
NGL Natural Gas Liquid
NGPA Natural Gas Policy Act
NGTF National Gay Task Force

NH New Hampshire
NHA National Homebuilders Association
NHCA National Hairdressers and Cosmetologists Association
NHI National Health Insurance
NHL National Hockey League
NHMA National Housewares Manufacturers Association
NHPA National Horseshoe Pitchers' Association
NHRA National Hot Rod Association

NHTSA National Highway Traffic Safety
Administration

Ni Nickel
NIA National Income Accounts
National Institute on Aging
NIAAA National Institute on Alcohol
Abuse and Alcoholism
NIAIS National Institute of Allergy
and Infectious diseases
NIAMDD National Institute of Arthritis,
Metabolism and Digestive
Diseases
NIASE National Institute for
Automotive Service
Excellence
NIC National Institute of
Corrections
NICAP National Investigations
Committee on Aerial
Phenomena
NICHD National Institute of Child
Health and human
Development
NIDA National Institute on Drug
Abuse
NIFO Next In, First Out
NIH National Institutes of Health
NILECJ National Institute of Law
Enforcement and Criminal
Justice
NIMH National Institute of Mental
Health
NIMPA National Independent Meat
Packers Association
NINCDS National Institute of
Neurological and
Communicative Disorders and
Stroke
NIOSH National Institute for
Occupational Safety and
Health
NIPA National Income and Products
Accounts

NIPPE	National Income Per Person Employed
NIS	National Institutes of Science
NISBCO	National Interreligious Service Board for Conscientious Objectors
NIT	National Invitational Tournament (Basketball)
	Negative Income Tax
NITL	National Industrial Traffic League
NIVT	National Invitational Volleyball Tournament
NJ	New Jersey
NJCAA	National Junior College Athletic Association
NL	National League (Baseball)
NLA	National Librarians Association
NLAA	National Legal Aid Association
NLC	National League of Cities
NLGI	National Lubricating Grease Institute
NLM	National Library of Medicine
NLN	National League for Nursing
NLRA	National Labor Relations Act
NLRB	National Labor Relations Board
NLSMB	National LiveStock and Meat Board
NLV	Net Liquidation Value
nm	Nonometer
NM	Nautical Mile
	New Mexico
NMA	National Microfilm Association
	National Micrographics Association
NMAB	National Materials Advisory Board
NMB	National Mediation Board
NMC	National Music Council
NMCS	National Military Command System

NMDA	National Motorcycle Dealers Association
NME	Noise Measuring Equipment
NMFC	National Motor Freight Classification
NMFS	National Marine Fisheries Service
NMFTA	National Motor Freight Traffic Association
NMLA	National Muzzle-Loading Association
NMNH	National Museum of Natural History
NMOS	N-channel Metal-Oxide-Silicon
NMP	Navigational Microfilm Projector
NMPA	National Music Publishers Association
NMPC	National Minority Purchasing Council
NMPS	Nautical Miles Per Second
NMR	Nuclear Magnetic Resonance
NMS	National Market System
NMTBA	National Machine Tool Builders Association
NN	Normal Null (Geodesy)
NNA	National Newspaper Association
NNP	Net National Product
NNR	New and Nonofficial Remedies
No	Nobelium
	Number
NOAA	National Oceanic and Atmospheric Administration
NOE	Nuclear Overhauser Effect
NOH	Notice of Opportunity for a Hearing (FDA)
NOI	Net Operating Income
NOJC	National Oil Jobbers Council
NOL	Naval Ordnance Laboratory
	Net Operating Loss
NORAD	NORth American air Defense command

NORML National Organization for the
Reform of Marijuana Laws
NORRA National Off Road Racing
Association
NOSG Naval Ordnance Systems
Command
NOSS National Oceanic Satellite
System
NOTAM NOTice to AirMen
NOW National Organization of
Women
Negotiable Order of Withdrawal
NOX Nitrous OXide

Np Neptunium
NP NeuroPsychiatry
Nitro Proved (Rifle Mark)
Nurse Practitioner
Nursing Procedure
npa Neutrons Per Absorption
NPA National Parking Association
Numbering Plan Area
NPC National Paddling Committee
National Press Club
NPCA National Paint and Coatings
Association
National Parks and
Conservation Association
National Pest Control
Association
NPD North Polar Distance
NPDES National Pollutant Discharge
Elimination System
npf Neutrons Per Fission
NPFFPA National Prepared Frozen Food
Processors Association
NPH Neutral-Protamine-Hagedorn
(Insulin)
Normal Pressure Hydrocephalus
NPK Nitrogen, Phosphate and Potash
NPN Non Protein Nitrogen
NPPC National Pork Producers Council
NPR National Public Radio
Net Protein Ratio

Nuclear Paramagnetic
Resonance
NPRA National Petroleum Refiners
Association
NPS National Parks Service
Naval Postgraduate School
North Polar Sequence
NPSH Net Positive Suction Head
(Pump)
NPTA National Paper Trade
Association
NPU Net Protein Utilization
NPV Net Present Value

NQR Nuclear Quadruple Resonance

NR Natural Rubber
NRA National Recovery
Administration
National Recreation Area
National Restaurant
Association
National Rifle Association
Noise-Reduction Amplifier
NRAB National Railroad Adjustment
Board
NRAO National Radio Astronomy
Observatory
NRB National Religious Broadcasters
NRC National Research Council
Noise Reduction Coefficient
Nuclear Regulatory Commission
NRDC Natural Resources Defense
Council
NREM NonRapid Eye Movement
NRHA National Retail Hardware
Association
NRHC National Rental Housing
Council
NRL Naval Research Laboratory
NRLCA National Rural Letter Carriers'
Association
NRMA National Retail Merchants
Association

NROTC	Naval Reserve Officer Training Corps
NRPA	National Recreation and Park Association
NRR	Net Reproduction Rate
NRS	National Recipient System
	Non-Rising Stem (Valve)
NRTA	National Retired Teachers Association
NRTWC	National Right To Work Committee
Ns	Nimbostratus (Clouds)
NS	Neurosurgery
NSA	Nashville Songwriters Association
	National Security Agency
	National Ski Association
	National Spiritualist Association
	National Student Association
NSAA	National Ski Areas Association
NSAC	National Society for Autistic Children
NSBA	National Small Business Association
NSC	National Security Council
NSCLC	National Senior Citizens Law Center
NSD	National Smooth Dancers
NSF	National Sanitation Foundation (Code)
	National Science Foundation
	Not Sufficient Funds
NSGA	National Sporting Goods Association
NSIA	National Security Industrial Association
NSLI	National Service Life Insurance
NSLL	National Savings and Loan League
NSM	National Soaring Museum
NSMR	National Society for Medical Research

NSNA National Student Nurse
Association
NSPA National Standard Parts
Association
NSPE National Society of Professional
Engineers
NSPS National Ski Patrol System
New Source Performance
Standards
NSSA National Senior Sports
Association
National Skeet Shooting
Association
NSSC Naval Ship Systems Command
Neutral Sulfite Semi-Chemical
NSSDA National Service Station
Dealers Association
NSSF National Shooting Sports
Foundation
NSSL National Severe Storms
Laboratory
NSTA National Science Teachers
Association
National Securities Traders
Association
NSWMA National Solid Waste
Management Association
NSWWP National Socialist White
Workers Party

Nt Niton
NT New Testament
NTA National Theatre
Administration
Nitrilotriacetate
NTC National Tax-limitation
Committee
NTE National Teacher Examination
NTGA National Traveler's Gasoline
Advisory
NTI Noise Transmission Impairment
NTIA National Telecommunications
and Information
Administration

NTID	National Technical Institute for the Deaf
NTIS	National Technical Information Service
NTMA	National Tile Manufacturers Association
NTO	National Tenants Organization
NTP	National Transportation Policy
	Normal Temperature and Pressure
NTRS	National Therapeutic Recreation Society
NTS	National Traffic System
	Not To Scale
NTSB	National Transportation Safety Board
NTSC	National Television System Committee
NTU	Nephelometric Turbidity Unit
	Number of Transfer Units
NUCA	National Utility Contractors Association
NUDETS	NUclear DETonationS
NUL	National Urban League
NUPOC	NUclear Propulsion Officer Candidate
NURE	National Uranium Resource Evaluation
NV	Nevada
NVACP	Neighborhoods, Voluntary Associations and Consumer Protection
NVC	Non Verbal Communication
NW	Narrow Width
NWA	National Wrestling Alliance
NWDS	National Water Data System
NWF	National Wildlife Federation
NWL	Naval Weapons Laboratory
NWPC	National Women's Political Caucus

NWS	National Weather Service
NWWA	National Water Well Association
NY	New York
NYA	National Youth Administration
NYC	National Youth Corps
	New York City
NYCE	New York Cotton Exchange
NYD	Not Yet Diagnosed
NYFE	New York Futures Exchange
NYIE	New York Insurance Exchange
NYME	New York Mercantile Exchange
NYSE	New York Stock Exchange

O	Orthodox
	Oxygen
OA	Overeaters Anonymous
OAA	Office of Accident Analysis
	Old Age Assistance
	Older Americans Act
	Oxaloacetate
OAJ	Opening Altitude Judgment (Parachuting)
OALAC	Older Americans' Legal Action Center
OALS	Office of Arid Land Studies
OAO	Orbiting Astronomical Observatory
OAP	Office of Antarctic Programs
OAPEC	Organization of Arab Petroleum Exporting Countries
OAR	Office of Aerospace Research
	OverAll Rate (Real Estate)
OAS	Organization of American States
	Oxygen Activated Sludge
OASDHI	Old-Age, Survivors, Disability and Health Insurance
OAU	Organization of African Unity

OB-GYN	OBstetrics-GYNecology
OBI	OmniBearing Indicator
OBM	Ordnance Bench Mark (Surveying)
OBO	Ore, Bulk, Oil (Merchant Ship)
OBS	Opera Ballet School
OBUs	Offshore Banking Units (Oil)
oc	Ohm-Centimeter
OC	Operating Characteristic (QA) Ordinary Capital
OCA	Office of Chief Accountant Office of Consumer Affairs
OCAW	Oil, Chemical and Atomic Workers international union
OCC	Order of Calced Carmelites
OCD	Office of Civil Defense
OCMS	Optimal Calling Measured Service (Telephone)
OCR	Office of Civil Rights Office of Coal Research Order of Cistercians Reformed (Trappists) Oscillating Cathode Ray
OCS	Officer Candidate School Outer Continental Shelf
OCT	Operational Cycle Time
OCTV	Open-Circuit TeleVision
OD	Doctor of Optometry Officer of the Day Organizational Development Outside Diameter Overdose Overdrawn Overdrive
ODECA	Organization of Central American States
OE	Offensive End (Football) Open End (Spinning Yarn)
OECD	Organization for Economic Cooperation and Development

OEDP Overall Economic Development
Program
OEEC Organization for European
Economic Cooperation
OEO Office of Economic Opportunity
OEP Office of Emergency Planning
OES Order of the Eastern Star

OF Outfield
OFCCP Office of Federal Contract
Compliance Programs
OFF Office For Families
OFM Order of Friars Minor
(Franciscans)
OFS Office of Field Services
Office of Foreign Secretary

OGE Opto-Galvanic Effect
OGO Orbiting Geophysical
Observatory

OH Ohio
O-H Omni-Horizon
ohc OverHead Camshaft
OHO Office of Hydrography and
Oceanography
ohv OverHead Valve

OI Operations Improvement
OIAJ Office for the Improvement of
the Administration of Justice
OIC Office of Industrial Cooperation
OIT Optimum Insulation Thickness
oiv Overhead Inlet Valve

OJ Orange Juice
OJAG Office of Judge Advocate General
OJARS Office of Justice Assistance,
Research and Statistics
OJT On the Job Training

OK Okay
Oklahoma

OL	On-Line
OLA	Office of Legislative Affairs
OLAS	Organization for Latin American Solidarity
OLMR	Organic Liquid-Moderated Reactor
OLP	Oxygen-Lime-Powder (Steel Process)
OLRT	On-Line Real-Time
OLS	Ordinary Least Squares (Stock Speculation)
OLTT	On-Line Teller Terminal
OLV	Orbital Launch Vehicle
O&M	Operations and Management
OMB	Office of Management and Budget
OMBE	Office of Minority Business Enterprise
OMC	Office of Munition Control
OMI	Oblates of Mary Immaculate
OMNI	Omnidirectional
OMPC	Overseas Military Personnel Charter
ON	Octane Number
ONA	Orthonitroaniline
ONAP	Office of Native American Programs
OND	Office of Neighborhood Development
ONI	Office of Naval Intelligence
ONP	Operating Nursing Procedures
ONR	Office of Naval Research
OOB	Off Off Broadway
OOD	Officer Of the Deck
OOP	Out Of Pocket
OP	Order of Preachers (Dominicans)
OPA	Office of Price Administration
OPC	Optical Particle Counter

OP&CMIA	Operative Plasterers' and Cement Masons' International Association
OPD	Optical Path Difference
OPE	Open Point Expanding (Bullet)
OPEC	Organization of Petroleum Exporting Countries
OPEI	Outdoor Power Equipment Institute
OPEIU	Office and Professional Employees International Union
OPIC	Overseas Private Investment Corporation
OPM	Office of Personal Management Other People's Money
OPP	Office of Pesticide Programs
OPT	Operation Prime Time (TV)
OPW	Orthogonalized Plane-Wave
OR	Olympic Record Operating Room Operations Research Oregon Outside Radius Own Recognizance
O&R	Ocean and Rail
ORB	Omnidirectional Radio Beacon
ORBIS	Orbiting Radio Beacon Ionosphere Satellite
ORC	Organized Reserve Corps
ORD	Ordnance
ORI	Octane Requirement Increase
ORP	Oxidation-Reduction Potential
ORS	Office of Revenue Sharing Orthopedic Research Society
ORT	Organization for Rehabilitation through Training
ORTS	Optimal Residence Telephone Service
ORV	Off-the-Road Vehicle
Os	Osmium

OS	Off Stage
	Operating Systems
	Operational Satellite
	Optical Scanning
O-S	Open Space
OSCAR	Orbiting Satellite Carrying Amateur Radio
OSD	Office of the Secretary of Defense
OSHA	Occupational Safety and Health Administration
OSM	Office of Surface Mining
OSO	Orbiting Solar Observatory
	Ore, Slurry, Oil (Merchant Ship)
OSS	Office of Strategic Services
OSTP	Office of Science and Technology Policy
OS&Y	Outside Screw and Yoke
OT	Occupational Therapy
	Old Testament
	Overtime
OTA	Office of Technology Assessment
	Output Transformerless Amplifier
OTB	Off-Track Betting
OTC	One-stop inclusive Tour Charter
	Over The Counter
OTEC	Ocean Thermal Energy Conversion
OTF	Other Than Fuel
OTHB	Over-The-Horizon Backscatter
OTIP	Office of Technical Information and Publications
OTP	Ocean Thermal Power
OTR	Over The Road
OTS	Office of Technical Services
	Officers Training School
	Orthotoluenesulfonamide
OTW	Over The Wing
OUAM	Order of United American Mechanics

OV	Orbiting Vehicle
OVR	Office of Vocational Rehabilitation
OW	Offering Wanted (Stock)
	Oil-immersed Water-cooled (Transformer)
OWL	Older Women's League
OWRT	Office of Water Research and Technology
OWS	Orbital Weapons System
OXO	Hydrocarboxylation
OYM	Outstanding Young Man
OZ	Ounce

P Pepper
Perishable
Phosphorus
Pa Pascal
Protactinium
PA Pennsylvania
Physician Assistant
Polar Atlantic (Air Mass)
Power of Attorney
Public Accountant
Public Address system
Purchasing Agent
PAA PolyAcrylic Acid
Professional Archery
Association
PAB Power-Assisted Brakes
PABA Para-AminoBenzoic Acid
PABST Primary Adhesively Bonded
Structure Technology
PABX Private Automatic Branch
eXchange
PAC Political Action Committee
PACE Professional and Administrative
Career Examination
Public And Community
Employment

PACER   Police Associated Citizens
Emergency Radio
PAD   Predicted Area of Danger
PADAR   PAssive Detection And Ranging
PADI   Professional Association of
Diving Instructors
PAGEOS   PAssive Geodetic Earth-
Orbiting Satellite
PAL   Phase ALternating system
Present Atmosphere Level
Programmable Array Logic
PAM   Plasma-Arc Machining
Polyacrylamide
Pulse Amplitude Modulation
PAMI   Performing Arts Management
Institute
PAN   (PeroxyAcetyl) (PolyAcrylo)
Nitril
PAO   Pro Athletes Outreach
PAP   Primary Atypical Pneumonia
PAPS   Phosphoaodenosinephospho-
sulfate
PAR   Perimeter Acquisition Radar
Precision Approach Radar
PARM   Party of the Mexican Revolution
PARS   Passenger Airline Reservation
System
PAS   Para-Amino Salicylic acid
Percussive Arts Society
Power-Assisted Steering
PAT   Preauthorized Automatic
Transfer
PATCO   Professional Air Traffic
Controllers Organization
PAU   Pan American Union
PAW   Plasma Arc Welding
PAX   Private Automatic eXchange
(Telephone)
PAYE   Pay As You Earn

Pb   Lead
PBs   Patrol Bombers

PBA PolyButyl Acrylate
Professional Bowlers
Association
PBAN PolyButadiene, AeryloNitrile,
acrylic acid
PBB PolyBrominated Biphenyls
PBD Polybutadiene
PBGC Pension Benefit Guaranty
Corporation
PBI Process Branch Indicator
Protein-Bound Iodine
PBM Plasma-Beam Machining
PBR Patrol Boat River
PBS Public Broadcasting Service
Public Buildings Service
PBX Private Branch eXchange
(Telephone)

pc Parsec
pC Picocurie
PC Petty Cash
Photocathode
Plasma Chromatography
Point of Curvature (Surveying)
Polar Continental (Air Mass)
Polycarbonate
Post Commander
Processing Conditions (Food)
Pulsating Current
Pulverized Coal
P-C Physical-Chemical
PCA Parachute Club of America
Polar Cap Absorption
Production Credit Association
PCAA Pacific Coast Athletic
Association
PCB Plenum Chamber Burning
Printed Circuit Board
PCC Point of Compound Curvature
Portland Cement Concrete
PCCs Product Customer Centers
PCCP Prestressed Concrete Cylinder
Pipe

PCE Personal Consumption
    Expenditure
  Potentially Compensable Event
  Pyrometric Cone Equivalent
PCG Phonocardiogram
PCJE Program on Criminal Justice
    and the Elderly
PCM Photo Chemical Machining
  Plug-Compatible Manufactures
  Porcelain Ceramic Mosaic
  Pulse Code Modulation
  Punched Card Machine
PCO Pest Control Operator
PCP Paired Cone Pigment
  Pentachlorophenol
  PhencyClidine hydrochloride
PCR Post-Conviction Review
PCS PerCent Solidified
  Permanent Change of Station
    (Military)
PCT Peak Central Temperature
PCUS Presbyterian Church in the
    United States
PCV Pack Cell Volume
PCWB Pulmonary Capillary Wedge
    Pressure

Pd Palladium
PD Per Diem
  Police Department
  Potential Difference
  Presidential Directive
  Public Defender
  Public Domain
PDA Patent Ductus Arteriosus
    (Heart)
  Post Deflection Acceleration
PDC Peak Discharge Current
PDD Past Due Date
PDE Position-Determining
    Equipment
PDF Powder Diffraction File
PDI Pilot's Direction Indicator

PDM	Physical Distribution Management
	Pulse Duration Modulation
PDMBD	PolyDiMethyl ButaDiene
PDP	Programmed Data Processor
PDQ	Pretty Damn Quick
PDS	PhotoDischarge Spectroscopy
PDT	Pacific Daylight Time
PE	Petroleum Engineer
	Physical Education
	Polyethylene
	Population Equivalent
	Potential Evapotranspiration
	Pressure-Electric
	Price-Earnings
	Professional Engineer
	Prospective Employer
	Protestant Episcopal
PEA	PolyEthyl Acrylate
PEF	Packaging Education Foundation
PEHA	PolyEthyl Hexyl Acrylate
PEI	Porcelain Enamel Institute
PEL	Permissible Exposure Limit
PEMA	PolyEthyl MethAcrylate
PEMEX	PEtroleos MEXicanos
PEN	Poets, playwrights, Editors, essayists and Novelists
PEP	Positron-Electron Project
	Precipitation Enhancement Project
	Public Employment Program
PER	Protein Efficiency Ratio
PERI	Platemakers Education and Research Institute
PERS	Public Employees Retirement System
PERT	Program Evaluation and Review Technique
PES	Photo Electron Spectroscopy
	Private Express Statutes
PET	PolyEthylene Terephthalate

PETN	PentaErythritol TetraNitrate
PETT	Positron Emission Transverse Tomography
pF	Picofarad
PF	Personal Foul (Basketball)
	Plain Face (Building)
	Power Factor
PFA	Pulverized Fuel Ash
PFC	Plow-Furrow-Cover (Waste)
	Private First Class
PFD	Personal, Fatigue, Delay
	Personal Flotation Device
	Power Flux Density
PFE	Photoferroelectric
PFET	Photo Field Effect Transistor
PFG	ProoF Gallon
PFI	Pipe Fabrication Institute
PFLP	Popular Front for the Liberation of Palestine
PFM	Pulse Frequency Modulation
PFP	Pet-Facilitated Psychotherapy
PG	Parental Guidance
	Pregnant
	Prosta Glandins
PGA	Professional Golfers' Association
PGH	Patrol Gunboat-Hydrofoil
PGP	Prepaid Group Practice (Medical)
	Pulsed Glide Path
PGR	Pencil GRoss
	Plant Growth Regulator
PGS	Propylene Glycol monoStearate
P-GTAW	Pulsed Gas Tungsten-Arc Welding
pH	Potential Hydrogen
PH	Purple Heart
P&H	Postage and Handling
PHA	Public Housing Administration
	Public Hunting Area

PHAs	Public Housing Agencies	
PHC	Personal Holding Company	
PHE	Public Health Engineer	
PHS	Public Health Service	
PI	Plasticity Index (Soil)	**211**
	Point of Intersection	
	(Surveying)	**PHAs-PLA**
	Polyisoprene	
	Profitability Index	
P/I	Principal/Interest	
PIA	Peripheral Interface Adapter	
	Post-Implementation Audit	
	Printing Industries of America	
PIB	Polyisobutylene	
PIC	Pilot-In-Command	
	Power Information Center	
PIE	Pulmonary Infiltrates with Eosinophilia	
PIN	Personal Identification Number	
	Police Information Network	
	Purveyors Identification Number	
PINO	Positive Input, Negative Output	
PIP	Programmable Integrated Processor	
PIS	Pesticides Information center	
PITI	Principal, Interest, Taxes and Insurance	
PIV	Peak Inverse Voltage	
PJ	Presiding Judge	
PJs	Pajamas	
pk	Peck	
PK	Pack	
	Psychokinesis	
PKs	Preachers' Kids	
PKU	Pheylketonuria	
PL	Promotion List	
P&L	Profit and Loss	
PLA	Programmable Logic Array	

PLF	Parachute Landing Fall
PLI	Practising Law Institute
PLO	Palestine Liberation Organization
PLS	Professional Legal Secretary
Pm	Promethium
PM	Phase Modulation
	Post Meridiem (After Noon)
	Preventive Maintenance
	Prime Minister
P/M	Powder Metallurgy
PMA	Pharmaceutical Manufacturers Association
	Phonograph Manufacturers Association
	PolyMethyl Acrylate
PMAA	PolyMethAcrylic Acid
PMAM	Polymethacrylamide
PMAN	Polymethacrylonitrile
PMBX	Private Manual Branch eXchange
PMH	Production per Man Hour
PMHP	Para-Menthane HydroPeroxide
PMI	Point of Maximum Impulse (Heart)
	Presidential Management Initiative
	Private Mortgage Insurance
PMLNA	Pattern Makers' League of North America
PMMA	PolyMethyl MethAcrylate
PMN	PolyMorphonuclear Nutrophil
PMOS	P-channel Metal-Oxide Silicon
PMR	Pacific Missile Range
	Polymerization of Monomer Reactants
	Pressure Modulator Radiometer
	Projection Micro-Radiography
PMS	Public Message Service
PMSG	Pregnant Mares Serum Gonadotrophin

PMSP Photon-counting
      MicroSpectroPhotometer
PMVI Periodic Motor Vehicle
      Inspection

PN Part Number
      Performance Number (Fuel
        Scale)
      Promissory Note
PNA Pakistan National Alliance
      PolyNuclear Aromatic
PNCC Polish National Catholic Church
PND Paroxysmal Nocturnal Dyspnea
PNdB Perceived Noise DeciBel
PNP Pediatric Nurse Practitioner

Po Polonium
PO Post Office
      Purchase Order
POA Pacific Ocean Area
      Police Officers Association
POC Port Of Call
      Production Operational
        Capability
      Products Of Combustion
POE Port Of Embarkation
      Port Of Entry
POGO Polar Orbiting Geophysical
        Observatory
POL Problem Oriented Language
        (Computer)
POP Printing-Out Paper
        (Photography)
      Proof Of Purchase
POQ Period, Order, Quantity
POR Payable On Receipt
POS Point Of Sale
POSS Passive Optical Satellite
        Surveillance
POT Point of Transaction
POV Privately Owned Vehicle
POW Pay Own Way
      Prisoner of War

POY   Polyester Oriented Yarn

PP   Pages
Peak-to-Peak
Polar Pacific (Air Mass)
Polypropylene
Porcelain Pavers

PPA   Phenylpropanolamine

PPB   Parts Per Billion
Planning, Programming and
   Budgeting

PPC   Plain Plaster Cornice
Points of Possible Collision

PPD   Purified Protein Derivative

PPF   Pellagra Preventative Factor

PPFA   Planned Parenthood Federation
   of America

PPGA   Personal-Producing General
   Agents (Insurance)

PPH   Paid Personal Holiday

ppi   Picks Per Inch (Weaving)

PPI   Pages Per Inch (Paper)
Patient Package Insert
Plan Position Indicator
Policy Proof of Interest
   (Insurance)

PPL   Penicilloyl-PolyLysine

PPLO   PleuroPneumonia-Like
   Organism

PPM   Parts Per Million
Pulse Position Modulation

PPP   Platelet-Poor Plasma

PPPA   Poison Prevention Packaging
   Act

PPPI   Precision Plan Position
   Indicator

PPPPI   Photographic Projection Plan
   Position Indicator

PPS   Page Printing System
Pulses Per Second

PPWL   Present Practice Waste Load

PPX   Professional Program eXchange

PQ Parti Quebecois (Canada)
Protein Quotient

Pr Praseodymium
PR Periodic Reverse (Plating)
Photo Reactivation (Radiation)
Primary Reference (Auto Fuel)
Public Relations
Puerto Rico
PRA Planetary Radio-Astronomy
PRC Peoples Republic of China
PRCA Professional Rodeo Cowboy's
Association
PRD Product Research and
Development
PRE Petroleum Refining Engineer
PREP Personal Radio Equipped Police
Pre-Retirement Education
Program
PRF Pulse Repetition Frequency
PRIME Precision Recovery Including
Maneuvering Entry (Space)
PRM Presidential Review
Memorandum
PROCO PROgrammed COmbustion
PROM Programmable Read-Only
Memory
PRP Platelet-Rich Plasma
PRR Pulse Repetition Rate
PRS Precipitate Reduction Sinter
(Metal)
PRSA Public Relations Society of
America
PRT Personal Rapid Transit

PS Polystyrene
Postscript
Pressure Switch
Public School
P&S Packers and Stockyards
Physicians and Surgeons
Purchase and Sale

PSA	Programmed Shutter and Aperture (Camera)
	Public Service Announcement
PSAC	President's Science Advisory Committee
	Production Switcher Automation System
PSAT	Preliminary Scholastic Aptitude Test
PSCs	Production Sharing Contracts
PSD	Pore Size Distribution (Ceramics)
	Power Spectral Density (Surface Texture)
	Prevention of Significant Deterioration
PSE	Pacific Stock Exchange
	Psychological Stress Evaluator
	Public Service Employee
psec	Picosecond
psi	Pounds per Square Inch
PSI	Personalized System of Instruction
psia	Pounds per Square Inch Absolute
PSIA	Professional Ski Instructors of America
psig	Per Square Inch Gage
PSP	Phenolsulfonphthalein
	Pointed Soft Point (Ammunition)
PSRA	Professional Ski Racers of America
PSRO	Professional Standards Review Organization
PST	Pacific Standard Time
pt	Pint
Pt	Platinum
PT	Patrol Torpedo (Boat)
	Physical Therapy
	Physical Training

Pipe Thread
Point
Point of Tangency
Potential Transformer
PTA Parent-Teachers' Association
Plasma Thromboplastin
    Antecedent
Pure Terephthalic Acid
PTC Phenyl ThioCarity or
    Phenylthiocarbamide
Plasma Thromboplastin
    Component
PTCA Private Truckers Council of
    America
PTFE Polytetrafluoroethylene
PTH ParaThyroid Hormone
PTI Post-Tensioning Institute
PTO Parent-Teacher Organization
Patent and Trademark Office
Please Turn Over
Power Take-Off
PTSA Parent-Teacher-Student
    Association
PTSD Post-Traumatic Stress Disorder
PTST Prime Time School Television
PTT Push To Talk
PTV Public TeleVision

Pu Plutonium
PU Pick-Up (Truck)
Propellant Utilization
PUC Public Utility Company
PUD Pick Up and Delivery
Planned Unit Development
PUMA Programmable Universal
    Machine for Assembly (Robot)
PUPs Performance Unit Plans
PURPA Public Utility Regulatory
    Policies Act
PUSH People United to Save Humanity
PUT Programmable Unijunction
    Transistor

PV	Par Value
	Pressure-Volume
	Prevention of Violence
PVA	PolyVinyl (Acetate) (Alcohol)
PVB	PolyVinyl Butyral
PVC	PolyVinyl Chloride
	Positive Crankcase Ventilation
	Premature Ventricular Contractions
PVD	ParaVisual Director (Instrument Flying)
	Peripheral Vascular Disease
PVDC	PolyVinyl DiChloride
PVEE	PolyVinyl Ethyl Ether
PVF	PolyVinyl (Fluoride) (Formal)
PVIBI	PolyVinyl IsoButyl ether
PVME	PolyVinylMethyl Ether
PVMK	PolyVinyl Methyl Ketone
PVP	Polyvinylpyrrolidone
PVT	Post Vintage Thoroughbred (Auto)
	Pressure, Volume, Temperature
PW	Packed Weight
PWA	Public Works Administration
PWBA	Plane-Wave Born Approximation (X-Ray)
PWM	Pulse-Width Modulation
PWP	Parents Without Partners
PWR	Pressurized Water Reactor
PX	Post eXchange
PZT	Lead Zirconate and Titanate
	Photographic Zenith Tube (Polar)

QA Quality Assurance
Q&A Question and Answer
QAC Quaternary Ammonium
Compound

QB Quarterback
QBTU Quad British Thermal Unit

QC Quality (Circle) (Control)
QCD Quantum ChromoDynamics
QCSHEE Quiet Clean Short-Haul
Experimental Engine

QE Queen Elizabeth (Ocean Liner)
QED Quantum ElectroDynamics
Quod Erat Demonstrandum
(Which was to be
demonstrated)
QFR Quarterly Financial Report
QHM Quartz Horizontal
Magnetometer

QOR Qualitative Operational
Requirement

QR	Quick Release
QSG	Quasi-Stellar Galaxy
QSO	Quasi-Stellar Objects
QSS	Quasi-Stellar Source
qt	Quart
QT	Quarry Tile
	(on the) QuieT
QTAM	Queued Telecommunications Access Method
QTOL	Quiet TakeOff and Landing
QWL	Quality-of-Work Life

R Rankin
Reformed
Registered (Patents)
Restricted (Movie)
Roentgen
Ra Radium
RA Radioactive
Rear Admiral
Regular Army
Research Assistantship
Rheumatoid Arthritis
Right Ascension
RAAF Royal Australian Air Force
RACE Random Access Computer
Equipment
RACES Radio Amateur Civil Emergency
Service
RACT Reasonably Available Control
Technology
rad Radian
RAD Radiation Accumulated Dose
Rear ADmiral
Relative Air Density
Rural Areas Development
RADA Royal Academy of Dramatic
Arts

RADAR	RAdio Detection And Ranging
RADEX	RADiological EXclusion area
RAF	Royal Air Force
RALU	Register and Arithmetic Logic Unit
RAM	Radio Attenuation Measurements
	Random Access Memory
	Recording AMmeter
	Reverse Annuity Mortgage
RAMP	Rural Abandoned Mines Program
RAP	Repair Allowance Percentage
RAPCON	Radar APproach CONtrol
RAPRA	Rubber And Plastics Research Association
RARE	Roadless Area Review and Evaluation
RARG	Regulatory Analysis Review Group
RAS	Rectified Air Speed
	Return of Activated Sludge
RATT	RAdio TeleTypewriter
RAWIN	RAdio WINd
RAX	Rural Automatic eXchange
Rb	Rubidium
RB	Reconnaissance Bomber
	Renegotiation Board
	Running Back (Football)
R&B	Rhythm and Blues
RBA	RiBo-nucleic Acid
	Running BAle
RBC	Red Blood Corpuscles
	Rotating Biological Contractor
RBE	Relative Biological Effectiveness
RBI	Runs Batted In (Baseball)
RBL	Lower Repair Bushing (Engine)
RBM	Reinforced Brick Masonry
RBP	Retinol Binding Protein
RBSN	Reaction Bonded Silicon Nitride
RBTIP	Residential Building Technology Innovations Program

RBU	Upper Repair Bushing (Engine)
RC	Radio Control
	Radix Complement
	Rapid Curing (Concrete)
	Record Changer
	Replacement Cost
	Resistance-Capacitance (Circuit)
	Roman Catholic
	Rubber-Cement
RCA	Radio Corporation of America
	Reformed Church in America
	Rodeo Cowboys Association
RCABV	Replacement-Cost-Adjusted Book Value
RCAF	Royal Canadian Air Force
RC&D	Resource Conservation and Development
RCDA	Religion in Communist-Dominated Countries
RCF	Remote Call Forwarding
RCIA	Retail Clerks International Association
RCL	Ruling Case Law
RCM	Radar Counter Measure
RCMP	Royal Canadian Mounted Police
RCP	Radar Chart Projector
	Reinforced Concrete Pipe
RCRA	Resource Conservation and Recovery Act
RCS	Ratio Control System (Coatings)
	Re-entry Control System (Space)
RCU	Retail Clerks Union
RCWP	Rural Clean Water Program
rd	Rod
RD	Registered Dietition
	Remaining Days
R&D	Research and Development
RDA	Received Data Available
	Recommended (Daily)
	(Dietary) Allowance
RDE	Receptor-Destroying Enzyme

RDF	Radio Direction Finder
	Refuse-Derived Fuel
RDH	Registered Dental Hygienist
RDP	Radar Data Processing
RDS	Respiratory Distress Syndrome
RDT&E	Research, Development, Test and Evaluation
Re	Rhenium
RE	Rare Earth
REA	Rural Electrification Administration
REACT	Radio Emergency Associated Communication Teams
READ	Real-time Electronic Access and Display
REAP	Rural Environmental Assistance Program
RECAT	Reduced Energy Consumption for commercial Air Transportation
RECOMP	REtrieval and COMPosition system (Computer)
REDCAP	Rail Expediting Daily Car Activity Program
REDCOM	REaDiness COMmand
REE	Rare Earth Elements
REG	Radioencephalogram
REIC	Radiation Effects Information Center
REITs	Real Estate Investment Trusts
REM	Radioactive EMission reading
	Rapid Eye Movement
	Roentgen Equivalent Man
REP	Roentgen Equivalent Physical unit
RER	Rough Endoplasmic Reticulum (Insulin)
RETMA	Radio Electronics Television Manufacturers Association
RETRF	Rural Electrification and Telephone Revolving Fund
REX	Regents EXternal degree program

RF Radio Frequency
Range-Finding
Representative Fraction (Globe Scale Ratio)
Right Fielder (Baseball)
Rigid Frame (Revolver)

RFB Recording For the Blind
RFC Radio Frequency Choke
Reconstruction Finance Corporation
RFD Rural Free Delivery
RFE Radio Free Europe
RFEHBP Retired Federal Employees Health Benefits Program
RFG Radar Field Gradient
RFI Radio Frequency Interference
RFK Robert Francis Kennedy
RFP Request For Proposal
RFS Render, Float and Set (Building)
RFU Ready For Use

Rh RHesus factor (Blood)
Rhodium
RH Relative Humidity
Rheostat
Right Hand
Rubber Heat (Wire)
Ruhrstahl (Iron Process)
RHD Relative Hepatic Dullness
RHEED Reflection High-Energy Electron Diffraction
RHI Range-Height Indicator (Radar)
RHIP Rank Has Its Privileges
rhm Roentgen-Hour-Meter
RHR Residual-Heat Remover (Exchanger)

RI Radio Inertial
Rhode Island
RIA Radioimmunoassay
RIAA Record Industry Association of America
RIC Rare-earth Information Center

RICO	Racketeering in Interstate COmmerce
RICU	Respiratory Intensive Care Unit
RID	Radio Intelligence Division (FCC)
RIE	Research In Education
RIF	Reading Is Fundamental
RIFM	Research Institute of Fragrance Materials
RIFT	Reactor-In-Flight Test
RIHANS	RIver and Harbor Aid to Navigation System (Coast Guard)
RIM	Reaction Injection Molding (Plastics)
RIP	Rest In Peace
RIR	Research Information and Retrieval
RISAR	Record Information Storage And Retrieval
RIT	Receiver Incremental Tuning
RL	Radio Liberty
R&L	Registration and Licensing
RLB	Right LineBacker (Football)
RLDS	Reorganized Latter-Day Saints
RLM	Rearward Launched Missile
RLR	Retired Lives Reserve (Insurance)
RLUF	Refundable Life Use Fee (Housing)
RM	Ream
	Ring Master
RMA	Radio Manufacturers Association
	Rubber Manufacturers Association
RMI	Radio Magnetic Indicator
RMS	Regional Market System
	Rural Manpower Service
RMSD	Root Mean Squared Deviation
RMSE	Root Mean Square Error
RMSF	Rocky Mountain Spotted Fever

Rn	Radon
RN	Registered Nurse
RNA	RiboNucleic Acid
RNC	Republican National Committee
RNP	Registered Nurse Practitioner
	Ribonucleoprotein
RNPA	Registered Nurses Professional Association
RNS	Religious News Service
RO	Reverse Osmosis
	Roll-On (Trailer Ship)
ROA	Reserve Officers Association
ROC	Republic Of China
	Reserve Officer Candidate
ROE	Rate of return On Equity
ROI	Return On Investment
ROM	Read-Only Memory
RON	Remain OverNight
	Research Octane Number (Oil)
ROP	Run Of the (Paper) (Press)
ROPS	Roll-Over Protective Structures (Tractors)
RO/RO	Roll On/Roll Off
ROS	Read-Only Store (Computer)
	Return On Sales
ROTC	Reserve Officers Training Corps
ROW	Right Of Way
RP	Received Pronunciation
	Reinforced Plastic
	Relief Pitcher
	Replacement Pilot
	Retinitis Pigmentosa
R/P	Reserve/Production Ratio
RPs	RePurchase agreements
RPA	Resources Planning Act
RPF	Renal Plasma Flow
RPG	Report Program Generator
RPI	Railway Progress Institute
	Relative Pollution Index
RPM	Revolutions Per Minute
RPO	Railway Post Office
	Rotating Parts Operation

RPR	Risk Premium Reinsurance
RPS	Renal Pressor Substance
	Revolutions Per Second
RPV	Relative Protein Value
	Remotely Piloted Vehicle
RQ	Respiratory Quotient
RQE	Responsive Quantum Efficiency
RR	Railroad
R&R	Range and Range-rate (Missile)
	Rest and Recuperation
RRA	Reserve Recognition Accounting
RRB	Railroad Retirement Board
RRC	Regular Route Carrier
RRIM	Reinforced Reaction Injection Molding (Plastics)
RRLL	Relative Rumble Loudness Level
RRM	Renegotiable Rate Mortgage
RRR	Return Receipt Requested
RRT	Rail Rapid Transit
RRWA	Retirement Research and Welfare Association
RS	Revised Statutes
	Right Safety (Football)
	Rising Stem (Valve)
RSFPP	Retired Serviceman's Family Protection Plan
RSJ	Rolled Steel Joist
RSP	Reconnaissance and Security Position (Military)
RSPO	Rail Services Planning Office (ICC)
RSR	Regular Sinus Rhythm (Heart)
RSRA	Rotor Systems Research Aircraft
RSROA	Roller Skating Rink Operators Association
RST	Residential Sub-surface Transformer

RSV Research Safety Vehicle
Revised Standard Version
(Bible)
RSVP *Répondez, S'il Vous Plait*
(Respond, If You Please)
Retired Senior Volunteer
Program

RT Rachet
Reading Test
Registered Technician
Right Tackle
Rise Time
Round Trip
RTA Real Time Analyzer
Real Tubular Acidosis
RTB Rural Telephone Bank
RTC Real-Time Clock
RTCA Radio Technical Commission for
Aeronautics
RTCM Radio Technical Commission for
Marine shipping
RTD Resistance-Temperature
Detector
RTE Ready To Eat
RTG Radioisotope Thermoelectric
Generator
RTL Resistor-Transistor Logic
RTM Resin Transfer Molding
(Plastics)
RTNDA Radio and Television News
Directors Association
RTOL Reduced TakeOff and Landing
RTPA Railway Travel Promotion
Agency
RTTY Radioteletypewriter
RTU Remote Terminal Unit

Ru Ruthenium
Rucus RUn CUtting and Scheduling
(Transit)
R/UDAT Regional/Urban Development
Assistance Team

RUF Resource-Utilization Factor

RV Recreational Vehicle
Rendezvous
Right Ventricle
R/V Re-entry Vehicle (Space)
Research Vessel
RVDA Recreational Vehicle Dealers
Association
RVIA Recreation Vehicle Industry
Association
RVOG Radio Voice Of the Gospel
RVP Red Veterinary Petrolatum

RW Rotary Wing (Airplane)
Rubber Wet (Wire)
R/W Read/Write
RWDSU Retail, Wholesale and
Department Store Union
RWL Raw Waste Load

Rx (Latin, Recipe) Take
(Prescription)
RYA Railroad Yardmaster of
America

S Saint
Salt
Siemens
Small
South
Sulfur

SA Salvation Army
Sinoatrial (Heart)
South America

SAA Society of American Archivists

SAAMI Sporting Arms and Ammunition Manufacturers Institute

SABE Society for Automation in Business Education

SABR Society for American Baseball Research

SAC Strategic Air Command

SACM Society of Authors and Composers of Music

SACRE Secure Airborne Control Radar Equipment

SAE Society of Automotive Engineers (Standard)

SAF Society of American Foresters

SAFE Security Assistance For the Elderly

SAG	Screen Actors Guild
SAHPS	Solar energy-Assisted Heat Pump System
SAIA	Survival of American Indians Association
SALT	Strategic Arms Limitation Treaty
SAM	Scanning Auger Microprobe
	Society for the Advancement of Management
	Surface to Air Missile
SAMA	Scientific Apparatus Manufacturers Association
SAMOS	Satellite And Missile Observation System
SAMSO	Space And Missile Systems Organization (Air Force)
SANS	Small Angle Neutron Scattering
SAP	Symbolic Assembly Program
SAR	Search And Rescue
	Sodium Absorption Ratio (Water)
	Submarine Advanced Reactor
	Synthetic Aperture Radar
SARs	Stock Appreciation Rights
SARAH	Search And Rescue And Homing
SAS	Safe Approach Speed
	Small Astronomy Satellite
SASE	Self-Addressed Stamped Envelope
SASI	System on Automotive Safety Information
SAT	Scholastic Aptitude Test
SATCO	Signal Automatic air Traffic COntrol
SATCOM	SATellite COMmunications
	Scientific And Technical COMmunications
SAW	Surface Acoustic-Wave
SAWA	Screen Advertising World Association
SAXAS	Scanning Automated X-ray Analysis Spectrometer

Sb Stilb
Antimony
SB *Scientiae Baccalaureus*
(Bachelor of Science)
Senate Bill
Simultaneous Broadcast
Stolen Bases (Baseball)
S/B Standby
SBA Small Business Administration
SBC Small Bayonet Cap
Southern Baptist Convention
SBICs Small Business Investment
Companies
SBLI Savings Bank Life
Insurance
SBP Survivor Benefit Plan
SBR Styrene-Butadiene Rubber

Sc Scandium
SC Scientific Communications
Signal Corps
Slow Curing (Concrete)
South Carolina
Spectre Coating (Camera Lens)
Sports Car
SCAN Senior Citizen Anti-crime
Network
SCAR Scientific Committee on
Antarctic Research
SCAT School and College Ability Test
Space Communications And
Tracking
SCC Small Claims Court
Squamous Cell Carcinoma
Stress-Corrosion Cracking
SCCA Sports Car Club of America
SCERP Stratospheric Cruise Emissions
Reduction Program
scf Standard Cubic Foot
SCF Stress Concentration Factor
scfm Standard Cubic Feet per Minute
SCG Screen Cartoonists Guild
SCID Severe Combined Immune
Deficiency

SCLC	Southern Christian Leadership Conference
SCLTFT	Space Charge Limited Thin Film Triode
SCN	Specification Change Notice
SCOOP	Scientific Computation Of Optimal Programs
SCOPE	Scientific Committee On Problems of the Environment
SCORE	Service Corps Of Retired Executives
	Signal Communication by Orbiting Relay Equipment
SCP	Senior Companion Program
	Single Cell Protein
SCR	SearCh Radar
	Signal Corps Radio
	Silicon Controlled Rectifier
SCRA	Smelter Control Research Association
SCRAM	Selective Combat Range Artillery Missile
SCS	Society for Computer Simulation
	Soil Conservation Service
	Spinal Cord Stimulation
SCSA	Standard Consolidated Statistical Area
SCUBA	Self-Contained Underwater Breathing Apparatus
SD	*Scientiae Doctor* (Doctor of Science)
	Service Drop (Cable)
	South Dakota
	Standard Deviation
	Surveillance Drone
	Suspended Dust
SDA	Seventh Day Adventists
SDB	Science Data Bank
SDF	Special Denatured Formula
SDP	Science Development Program
SDR	Standard Dimension Ratio
SDRs	Special Drawing Rights

SDS	Sodium Dodycyl Sulfate
	Special Distress Signal
	Students for a Democratic Society
SDWA	Safe Drinking Water Act

Se	Selenium
SE	Successful Efforts
SEA	Science and Education Administration
SEAC	(National Bureau of) Standards Eastern Automatic Computer
SEAL	SEa Air Land (Military)
SEARCH	System for Electronic Analysis and Retrieval of Criminal Histories
SEASAT	SEA SATellite
SEATO	SouthEast Asia Treaty Organization
sec	Second
SEC	Secondary Electron Conduction
	Securities Exchange Commission
	Simple Electronic Computer
	Special Event Charter
SECO	SEquential COntrol (Teletype)
	Sustainer Engine Cut Off (Space)
SED	Skin Erythema Dose
SEDCOM	Simulated EDucational COMputer
SEE	Society of Explosives Engineers
SEG	Screen Extras Guild
	Society of Exploration Geophysicists
SEIA	Solar Energy Industries Association
SEIU	Service Employees International Union
SEM	Scanning Electron Microscope
SEMA	Specialty Equipment Manufacturers Association
SEMI	Semiconductor Equipment and Materials association

SEOG	Supplemental Education Opportunity Grant
SEP	Simplified Employee Pension Plan
	Solar Electric Propulsion
SERF	Study of Energy Release in Flares (Solar)
SERI	Solar Energy Research Institute
SES	Standards Engineering Society
	Surface Effect Ship
SET	Simulated Emergency Test (Radio)
	Solar Energy Thermionic
SETI	Search for Extra-Terrestrial Intelligence
SF	Stability Factor
	Structural Foam (Plastics)
SFA	Single Function Appliance
SFAAPWIU	Stove, Furnace and Allied APpliance Workers' International Union
SFAS	Statement of Financial Accounting Standards
SFPM	Surface Feet Per Minute
SFWA	Science Fiction Writers of America
SGA	Substantial Gainful Activity
SGHW	Steam Generating Heavy Water
SGLI	Servicemen's Group Life Insurance
SGO	Surgeon General's Office
SGOT	Serum Glutamic Oxaloacetic Transaminase
SGPT	Serum Glutamic Pyruvic Transaminase
SH	Scleroscope Hardness
	Serum Hepatitis
SHA	Sidereal Hour Angle
SHAPE	Supreme Headquarters, Allied Powers, Europe

SHARP SHips Analysis and Retrieval
Project
SHF Super High Frequency
SHM Simple Harmonic Motion
shp Shaft HorsePower

Si Silicon
SI Sedimentation Index
Specific Impulse
Station Identification
International System of units
SIA Securities Industry Association
Semiconductor Industry
Association
SIAM Society for Industrial and
Applied Mathematics
SIBI Survivor Income Benefit
Insurance
SIC Specific Inductive Capacitor
Standard Industrial
Classification
SID Slew-Induced Distortion (Audio)
Sudden Ionospheric Disturbance
(Sun)
SIDS Sudden Infant Death Syndrome
SIF Sound Intermediate Frequency
SIG Special Interest Group
SIMPP Society of Independent Motion
Picture Producers
SIMS Secondary Ion Mass
Spectrometer
SINS Shipboard Inertial Navigation
System
SIPC Securities Industry Protection
Corporation
SIPI Scientists' Institute for Public
Information
SIR Specific Inductive Resistance
Submarine Intermediate
Reactor
SIT Self-Induced Transparency
(Optics)
Silicon-Intensified Target
(Vidicon Tube)

SIU	Seafarers International Union
	Special Investigation Unit
SJ	Society of Jesus (Jesuits)
	Soldered Joint (Plumbing)
SJD	Doctor of Juridical Science
SKU	Stock Keeping Unit
S/L	Sidelever (Rifle)
S&L	Savings and Loan
SLAM	Supersonic Low Altitude Missile
SLAR	Side-Looking Airborne Radar
SLBM	Submarine Launched Ballistic Missile
SLC	SearchLight Control (Radar)
	Social Learning Curriculum
SLCM	Sea-Launched Cruise Missile
SLE	Systematic Lupus Erythematosus
SLF	Straight Line Frequency
SLIC	Selective Listing In Combination (Computer)
SLMA	Student Loan Marketing Association (Sallie Mae)
SLP	Systematic Layout Planning
SLR	Single Lens Reflex (Camera)
SLT	Solid Logic Technology
SLV	Space Launch Vehicle
Sm	Samarium
SM	*Scientiae Magister* (Master of Science)
	Strategic Missile
SMA	Shielded-Metal Arc
SMACNA	Sheet Metal and Air Conditioning Contractors National Association
SMAS	Society for the Maintenance of the Apostolic See
SMAW	Shielded Metal-Arc Welding
SMC	Sheet Molding Compound
	Small Magellanic Cloud

SMD	Doctor of Sacred Music
SME	Society of Manufacturing Engineers
	Solar Mesospheric Satellite
SMI	Static Memory Interface
	Supplementary Medical Insurance
SMOW	Standard Mean Ocean Water
SMPTE	Society of Motion Picture and Television Engineers
SMS	Synchronous Meteorological Satellite
SMSA	Standard Metropolitan Statistical Area
SMSS	Surface Mining Simulation System
SMT	Ship Mean Time
SMWIA	Sheet Metal Workers' International Association
SMY	Solar Maximum Year
Sn	Tin
SN	Serial Number
	Signal-to-Noise
	Sporting News
SNA	Student Naval Aviator
SNAFU	Situation Normal—All [Fouled] Up
SNAME	Society of Naval Architects and Marine Engineers
SNAP	Stylized NAtural-language Processor
SNCC	Student Nonviolent Coordinating Committee
SNF	Skilled Nursing Facility
SNFCC	Shippers National Freight Claim Council
SNG	Substitute Natural Gas
SNO	Substitute Natural Oil
SNOBOL	StriNg Oriented symBOlic Language
SNR	SuperNova Remnant
SNU	Solar Neutrino Unit

SO	Shop Order
	Standing Order
	Strike-Outs
SOCMA	Synthetic Organic Chemical Manufacturers Association
SOF	Sound On Film
SOI	Structure Of Intellect
SOLAS	Safety Of Life At Sea
SOLE	Society Of Logistics Engineers
SONAR	SOund NAvigation Ranging
SOP	Standard Operating Procedure
	Statement Of Policy
SOPAC	SOuth PACific
SOR	Specific Operational Requirement
SOS	(International distress code; no actual initials)
	Senior Opportunities and Services
	Silicon On Sapphire
SOTA	State Of The Art
SOx	Sulfur OXide
SP	Sidepull (Bicycle)
	Station Point (Drafting)
	Stop Payment
S&P	Standard and Poor's index
SPAN	Solar Particle Alert Network
SPAR	Soil-Plant-Atmosphere Research
SPARS	*Semper PARatuS* (Always Ready, Women's Coast Guard Reserve)
SPCA	Serum Prothrombin Conversion Accelerator
	Society for the Prevention of Cruelty to Animals
SPCC	Society for the Prevention of Cruelty to Children
SPEBQSA	Society for the Preservation and Encouragement of Barbershop Quartet Singing in America

SPEDY	Summer Program for Employment Development for Youth	
SPEE	Society for the Promotion of Engineering Education	
SPF	Sun Protection Factor	**241**
sp gr	SPecific GRavity	
SPI	Society of the Plastics Industry	**SPEDY-SRC**
SPL	Sound Pressure Level	
SPLA	Specific Price-Level Accounting	
SPNS	Standards of Performance for New Sources (Power)	
SPOBS	SPecial OBServers (Military)	
SPOT	Satellite POsitioning and Tracking	
SPP	Speech Privacy Potential (Building)	
SPPs	Simplified Pension Plans	
SPR	SPRingfield (Rifle)	
SPS	Solar Photovoltaic Act	
	Solar Power Satellites	
	Symbolic Programming System (Computer)	
SPUR	Space Power Unit Reactor	
SPX	Stepped Piston CROSSover (Engine)	
SQ	Social Quotient	
	Status Quo	
sr	Steradian	
Sr	Strontium	
SR	Sarcoplasmic Reticulum (Muscle)	
	Scanning Radiometer	
	Senior	
SRA	Society of Real Estate Appraisers	
	Station Representatives Association	
	Supplemental Retirement Annuity	
SRC	Solvent Refined Coal	

SRI	Ski Retailers International
SRM	Standard Reference Materials (Surface Texture)
SRMSA	Southern Rocky Mountain Ski Association
SRO	Self-Regulatory Organization Standing Room Only
SRP	Suggested Retail Price
SRS	Scoliosis Research Society
SRT	Solids Retention Time (Wastewater)
SRTA	Stationary Reflector/Tracking Absorber (Solar)
SRWL	Standard Raw Waste Load
SS	Saints
	Same Size (Printing)
	Selective Service
	Shortstop
	Skywave-Synchronized
	Solid State
	Steamship
	Sugar Snap (Peas)
	Sunday School
S/S	Super Stock (Auto)
SxS	Side by Side
SSA	Soaring Society of America Social Security Administration
S/SA	Super Stock Automatic (Auto Transmission)
SSAP	Statement of Standard Accounting Practices
SSB	Single SideBand
SSC	Senior Service College Super Spectre Coating (Camera Lens)
SSD	Saturated Surface Dry (Concrete)
SSDI	Social Security Disability Insurance
SSI	Standards Starts Index (Horse Racing) SubSod Injection (Waste)

SSIE	Smithsonian Science Information Exchange
SSIG	Student State Incentive Grant
SSM	Surface-to-Surface Missile
SSN	Social Security Number
SSR	Secondary Surveillance Radar Solid State Relay
SSRC	Social Science Research Council
SSS	Selective Service System Specific Soluble (Capsular poly) Saccharide
SST	SuperSonic Transport
ST	Short Tour Surface Trench
S-T	Semi-Trailer
STAMP	Small Tactical Aerial Mobility Platform
STAR	Self-Testing And Repairing
STC	Sensitivity-Time Control (Radar) Single Trip Container Sound Transmissions Class
STCs	Stock Trust Certificates
STCC	Standard Transportation Commodity Code
STCR	Systems, Test and Checkout Reports (Space, "Streetcar")
STD	Doctor of Sacred Theology Sexually Transmitted Disorder Skin Test Dose
STEM	Shaped-Tube Electrolytic Machining
STEP	Selective Traffic Enforcement Program
STEPS	Solar Thermionic Electric Power System
STIP	Study of Travelling Interplanetary Phenomena
STL	Licentiate in Sacred Theology Studio-Transmitter Link
STOL	Short TakeOff and Landing
STORET	STOrage and RETrieval (Computer)

STP	Standard Temperature and Pressure
STPP	Sodium TriPolyPhosphate
STRAP	Simultaneous Transmission and Reception of Alternating Pictures (TV)
STRESS	STRuctural Engineering System Solver
STS	Serologic Test for Syphilis
	Ship To Shore
	Space Transportation System
STSR	Stepped-Temperature Stress-Rupture (Ceramics)
STTF	Solar Thermal Test Facility
STV	Subscription TeleVision
S/U	Suture
SUM	Surface-to-Underwater Missile
SUN	Solar Utilization Network
	Standard Units and Nomenclature (IUPAP)
sv	Side Valve
SV	Saves (Baseball)
SVC	Static Var Control
SVI	Sludge Volume Index
SVR	Security Verification Requirement
SW	Short Wave
SWAC	(National Bureau of) Standards Western Automatic Computer
SWAP	Society of Wang Applications and Programs
SWAPO	South West Africa People's Organization
SWAT	Special Weapons And Tactics force
swb	Short WheelBase (Auto)
SWC	Solar Wind Composition
	Special Weapons Center
SWE	Society of Women Engineers
SWECS	Small Wind-Energy Conversion System (Windmill)

SWG (imperial) Standard Wire Gage
SWL Short Wave Listener
SWP Socialist Workers Party
SWR Standing Wave Ratio

SYD Sum-of-the-Years-Digits
SYE Square Yards Equivalent

T	Temperature
	Tera
	Tesla (Magnetic Flux)
	Transformer
Ta	Tantalum
TA	Teaching Assistantship
	Transactional Analysis
	TransAm (Auto)
	Travel Agent
	Tropical Atlantic (Air Mass)
T&A	Tonsillectomy and Adenoidectomy
TAA	Transit Advertising Association
	Transportation Association of America
TAB	Technology Assessment Board
	Traffic Audit Bureau
	Typhoid, paratyphoid A, paratyphoid B (Vaccine)
TABS	Television Auxiliary Broadcast Service
TAC	Tactical Air (Command) (Control)
	TriAllyl Cyanurate
TACAMO	TAke Charge And Move Out

TACAN	TACtical Air Navigation
TACRV	Tracked Air-Cusion Research Vehicle (Mass Transit)
TAD	Telephone Answering Device
TADARS	Target Acquisitions/Designation Aerial Reconnaissance System
TADS	Tactical Air Defense System
TAG	Technique Avant-Garde (Auto) Trans-Atlantic Geotraverse
TALCOR	Transponder Array Location by CO-planar Ranges (Ocean)
TANU	Tanganyika African National Union
TAP	Tackled Attempting to Pass (Football)
TAPPI	Technical Association of the Pulp and Paper Industry
TAR	Training and Administration of the Reserve
TARA	Terrain Avoidance RAdar
TARP	Tunnel And Reservoir Plan
TAS	Tax Administration System (IRS Computer) Telephone Answering Service True Air Speed
TASH	Technology ASsessment of Hail
TASI	Time-Assignment Speech Interpolation (Telephone)
TASS	Telegraphnoye Agentstvo Sovyetskovo Soyuza (Soviet News Agency)
TASVAL	Tactical Aircraft effectiveness and SurVivAbiLity in close air support anti-armor operations
TAT	Thematic Apperception Test Toxin-AntiToxin
Tb	Terbium
TB	Tailback (Football) Terminal Board Tuberculosis
TBA	Tires, Batteries and Accessories To Be Announced

TBD	To Be Determined
TBM	Tunnel Boring Machine
TBP	TriButyl Phosphate
TBPC	TertButyl-P-Cresol
TBS	Tribromosalicylanilide
	(Antiseptic)
Tc	Technetium
TC	Tax Court
	Time Constant
	Top Center (Auto)
	Torque Converter
	Total Carbon
	Trip Coil
	Troop Carrier
	Tropical Continental (Air Mass)
T/C	Thermocouple
TCs	Trust Certificates
TCA	Technical Corrections Act (Tax)
	Television Critics Association
	Terminal Control Area
	Tri (Carboxylic) (Chloroacetic)
	Acid
TCAM	TeleCommunications Access
	Method
TCAPE	Truck Computer Analysis of
	Performance and Economy
TCBM	TransContinental Ballistic
	Missile
TCC	Triclocarban (Antiseptic)
	Troop Carrier Command
TCE	Tax Credit for the Elderly
	Temperature Coefficient
	of Expansion
	Trichloroethylene
TCF	Trillion Cubic Feet
TCM	ThermoChemical Machining
TCP	Traffic Control Plans
TCR	Temperature Coefficient of
	Resistance
TCS	Transmission Controlled Spark
	Transportation Control System
TCTO	Time Compliance Technical
	Order

TD Tardive Dyskinesia
Technical Draw (Boxing)
Total Depth
Touchdown
Treasury Decisions (Law)
TDs Trust Deeds
TDC Top Dead Center (Auto)
TDI Temporary Disability Insurance
Toluene DiIsocyanate
TDM Time Division Multiplexing
(Traffic)
TDN Total Digestible Nutrient
(Crops)
TDP Technical Development Plan
TDR Transfer of Development Rights
TDS Time-Delay Spectrometry
Transmitter Data Strobe
TDY Temporary DutY

Te Tellurium
TE Tight End (Football)
Top Eliminator (Drag Racing)
Touring Exchange
Transverse Electric
TEA Transversely Excited
Atmosphere (Laser)
Tunnel Emission Amplifier
TEAC TetraEthylAmmonium Chloride
TECA Temporary Emergency Court of
Appeals
TEDS Time Encoded Digital Speech
TEFC Totally Enclosed Fan-Cooled
(Motor)
TEL TetraEthyl Lead
TEM Total Energy Management
Transmission Electron
Microscope
TEMA Tubular Exchanger
Manufacturers Association
TENS Transcutaneous Electrical
Nerve Stimulator
TEPP TetraEthyl PyroPhosphate
TESA Television and Electronic
Service Association

TESOL Teachers of English to Speakers of Other Languages
TEST Thesaurus of Engineering and Scientific Terms
TET Thermometric Enthalpy Titrations
TEV Today's English Version (Good News Bible)

TF Task Force
Transfer Factor
TFC Total Fixed Cost
TFCS Treasury Financial Communications System
TFFET Thin Film Field-Effect Transistor
TFT Thin Film Transistor
TFX Tactical Fighter eXperimental (Plane)

TG Task Group
Thryoglobulin
Tropical Gulf (Air Mass)
T&G Tongue and Groove
TGA ThermoGravimetric Analysis
TGB Temporary GuideBase (Oil)
TGC Total Groove Contact (Records)
Travel Group Charter
TGIF Thank God It's Friday
TGS Transcontinental Geophysical Society

Th Thorium
THAM Tris (Hydroxymethyl) Amino Methane
THC Tetrahydrocannabinal
THD Total Harmonic Distortion
THI Temperature-Humidity Index
THM Trihalomethanes

Ti Titanium
TIA Transitory Ischemic Attack (Stroke)

TIAA Teachers Insurance and
Annuity Association
TIBA TriIodoBenzoic Acid
TIF True Involute Form (Gears)
TIG Tungsten Inert Gas (Welding)
TIM Transient InterModulation
TIP Tax-based Incomes Policy
Toxicology Information
Program
TIR Total Indicator Reading
(Transmission)
Total Internal Reflection
TIROS Television and InfraRed
Observation Satellite
TIS Technical Information Services
TISA The Institute for Safety
Analysis
TIT Turbine Inlet Temperatures
(Ceramics)
TIU Telecommunications
International Union

TK To Come (Printing)
TKA ThermoKinetic Analysis
TKD Tokodynamometer
TKG Tokodynagraph
TKO Technical Knock Out (Boxing)
TKPP TetraPotassium PyroPhosphate

Tl Thallium
TL Technical Loss (Boxing)
Truck Load
Trunk Line
TLB The Living Bible
TLC Taxed Less Certificate
Tender Loving Care
Theoretical Length of Cut (Corn)
Thin Layer Chromatography
Total Lung Capacity
Transmission-Line Cable
TLD Thermal Luminescent
Dosimeter (Radiation)

TLSP Transponder Location by
Surface Position (Ocean)

Tm Thulium
TM Tinnitus Masker (Ear)
Trademark
Transcendental Meditation
Transverse Magnetic
TMA Toy Manufacturers of America
Truck-Mounted Attenuator
TMAO TriMethylAmine Oxide
TMGs Timber Management Groups
TMI Three Mile Island
TMIC Toxic Materials Information
Center
TMJ Temporo-Mandibular Joint (Jaw)
TMMC TetraMethyl ammonium
Manganese Chloride
TMPH Ton-Mile Per Hour (Heavy Tires)
TMU Time Measurement Unit
TMV Tobacco Mosaic Virus
TMX Tandem Mirror eXperiment
TMY Typical Meteorological Year

tn Ton
TN Tennessee
Trade Name
TNC TransNational Company
TNE TransNational Enterprise
TNG The Newspaper Guild
TNT (Trinitrotoluene) (Trinitrotoluol)

TO Take Off
Turnover
T/O Target of Opportunity
TOC Television Operating Center
Total Organic Carbon
TOCS Terminal-Oriented Computer
System
TOD Total Oxygen Demand
TOE Tons of Oil Equivalent
Total Operating Expense

TOFC	Trailer-On-Flat Car
TOP	Trade Opportunities Program
TOPICS	Traffic Operations Program for Increasing Capacity and Safety
TOS	Tape Operating System
	Tiros Operational Satellite
TOSCA	TOxic Substances Control Act
TOT	Time On Target
TOZ	Troy Ounce
TP	Thermoplastic
	Toilet Paper
	Tower Proof (Gunpowder)
	Tropical Pacific (Air Mass)
	Turning Point (Surveying)
TPC	Tournament Players Championship (Golf)
TPG	Thermal Performance Guidelines
tph	Tons Per Hour
TPI	Teeth Per Inch
	Threads Per Inch (Screws)
	Travel Price Index
TPM	Trigger Price Mechanism
TPN	Total Parenteral Nutrition
	TriPhosphopyridine diNucleotide
TPR	Temperature Pressure Relief (Water Heater Valve)
	Temperature, Pulse and Respiration
	Trigger-Pulse Repeater
TPT	TelePrompTer
TPTZ	TriPyridyl-s-TriaZine
TPV	Thermal PhotoVoltaic converter
TR	Total Revenue
	Transmit-Receive
TRA	Tax Reform Act
	Thoroughbred Racing Association
	Tire and Rim Association

TRAAC Transit Research And Altitude
Control
TRACON Terminal Radar Approach
CONtrol
TRADEX Tracking RADar, EXperimental
TRADOC TRAining and DOCtrine
command (Army)
TRASOP Tax Reduction Act employee
Stock Ownership Plan
TRB Transportation Research Board
TRF Tuned Radio Frequency
TRHD Twin-Row High-Density (Trees)
TRIP The Road Information Program
Thunderstorm Research
International Program
TRL Transistor-Resistor Logic
TRS Teleoperator Retrieval System
Total Reduced Sulfur
TRSA Terminal Radar Service Area
TRSB Time Reference Scanning Beam
TRU Turbidity Reducing Unit
TRUMP Target Radiation Measurement
Program
TRUST Television Relay Using Small
Terminals

TS Tensile Strength
Test Solution
Thermosetting (Plastics)
Tilt and Shift (Camera Lens)
TSA Training for Service Abroad
TSH Thyrotrophin Stimulating
Hormone
TSI Timber Stand Improvement
TSM Transportation System
Management
TSO Technical Standards Orders
Time Sharing Option
TSP TriSodium Phosphate
TSS Time-Sharing System
Total Suspended Solids
Twin-Screw Steamer
TSTAs Tumor-Specific Transplantation
Antigens

TT	Tourist Trophy (Motorcycling)
TTA	Thenoyl Trifluoro Acetone
TTG	Time To Go
TTH	Ten-Thousandth of an Hour
	ThyroTrophic Hormone
TTL	Through-The-Lens (Camera)
	Transistor-Transistor Logic
TTP	ThymidineTriPhosphate
TTS	TeleType System
TTT	Triethyl Trimethylene Triamine
TUC	Trades Union Congress (Britain)
TUR	TransUrethral Resection
TURP	TransUrethral Resection of Prostrate
TV	TeleVision
	Test Vehicle
TVA	Tennessee Valley Authority
TVB	TeleVision Bureau of advertising
TVC	TeleVision Commercial
	Thrust Vector Control (Space)
	Total Variable Cost
TVI	TeleVision Interference
TVIG	TeleVision Inertial Guidance
TVM	Transistor VoltMeter
TVOM	Transistor Volt-OhmMeter
TVP	Textured Vegetable Protein
TVR	TeleVision Recording
TVS	Thermostatic Vacuum Switch (Auto)
TW	Technicial Win (Boxing)
	Traveling Wave
TWI	Training Within Industry
TWIU	Tobacco Workers International Union
TWT	Traveling-Wave Tube (Transmitter)
TWU	Transport Workers Union
TWUA	Textile Workers Union of America

U	Uranium
UA	United Association of journeymen and apprentices of the plumbing and pipe fitting industry
UAE	United Arab Emirates
UAHC	Union of American Hebrew Congregations
UAM	Underwater-to-Air Missile
UAMS	Upper Atmosphere Mass Spectrometer
UANC	United African National Council
UAR	United Arab Republic
UARS	Upper Atmosphere Research Satellite
UART	Universal Asynchronous Receiver Transmitter
UAW	United Automobile, aerospace and agricultural implement Workers
UBC	Uniform Building Code United Brotherhood of Carpenters and joiners
UBCWA	United Brick and Clay Workers of America

UBI	Ultraviolent Blood Irradiation
	Unrelated Business Income
UBL	United Basketball League
UBOA	United Boat Owners of America
UC	Undercharge
	Undercurrent
	Unit Call
UCAR	Union of Central African Republics
UCC	Uniform Commercial Code
	United Church of Christ
	Universal Copyright Convention
UCLGWIU	United Cement, Lime and Gypsum Workers International Union
UCMJ	Uniform Code of Military Justice
UCR	Uniform Crime Reports
	Usual, Customary and Reasonable (Medical Fees)
UCS	UnConditional Stimulus
	Union of Concerned Scientists
UDAG	Urban Development Action Grant
UDC	United Daughters of the Confederacy
	Universal Decimal Classification
UDEAC	Union Douanière et Économique de l'Afrique Centrale (Central African Customs and Economic Union)
UDEAO	Customs Union of West African States
UDFFC	Unity-Displacement-Factor Frequency Changer
UDIA	United Dairy Industry Association
UDITPA	Uniform Division of Income for Tax Purposes Act
UDMH	Unsymmetrical DiMethyl Hydrazine
UDP	Uridine DiPhosphate
UDPG	Uridine DiPhospho Glucose

UE	United Electrical, radio and machine workers
UF	Underground Feeder (Cable)
UFAC	Upholstered Furniture Action Council
UFC	Unrestricted Frequency Changer
UFO	Unidentified Flying Object
UFW	United Farm Workers
UFWA	United Furniture Workers of America
UG	Universal Generalization
UGCW	United Glass and Ceramic Workers
UGDP	University Group Diabetes Program
UGI	Unity-Gain Indicator (Audio)
UGPA	Undergraduate Grade Point Average
UGW	United Garment Workers
UHC	Ultra High Carbon (Steel)
UHCMW	United Hatters, Cap and Millinery Workers
UHF	Ultra High Frequency
UHI	Universal Health Insurance
UHTREX	Ultra-High-Temperature Reactor EXperiment
UHV	Ultra High Vacuum
UID	Universal IDentification number
UIU	Upholsterers' International Union
UJT	UniJunction Transistor
UK	United Kingdom
UKC	United Kennel Club
UL	Underwriters Laboratories
U/L	Underlever (Rifle)
ULA	Uncommitted Logic Array

ULCA	United Legal Christian Association
	United Lutheran Church in America
ULD	Unit Load Device
UMC	United Methodist Church
UMP	Uridine MonoPhosphate
UMS	Universal Maintenance Standards
UMT	Universal Military Training
UMTA	Urban Mass Transportation Administration
UMWA	United Mine Workers of America
UN	United Nations
UNC	UNified Course (Screws)
UNCF	United Negro College Fund
UNCHE	United Nations Conference on the Human Environment
UNCLOS	United Nations Conference on the Law Of the Sea
UNCTAD	United Nations Conference on Trade And Development
UNDOF	United Nations Disengagement Observer Force in the Golan Heights
UNEF	UNified Extra Fine (Screw Threads)
	United Nations Emergency Force
UNEP	United Nations Environment Program
UNESCO	United Nations Educational, Scientific and Cultural Organization
UNF	UNified Fine (Screws)
UNFPA	United Nations Fund for Population Activities
UNH	Uranyl Nitrate Hexahydrate
UNHCR	United Nations High Commissioner for Refugees

UNICEF	United Nations International Children's Emergency Fund
UNIDO	United Nations Industrial Development Organization
UNIFIL	United Nations Interim Force In Lebanon
UNITA	Uniao Nacional para a Independencia Total de Angola (National Union for the Total Independence of Angola)
UNITAR	United Nations Institute for Training And Research
UNITY	United National Indian Tribal Year
UNIVAC	UNIVersal Automatic Computer
UNLF	Uganda National Liberation Front
UNRRA	United Nations Relief and Rehabilitation Administration
UNRWA	United Nations Relief and Works Agency
UOC	Ultimate Operational Capacity
UOJC	Union of Orthodox Jewish Congregations
UP	Utilizable Protein
UPA	Uniform Partnership Act
UPC	Universal Product Code
UPCUSA	United Presbyterian Church in the United States of America
UPGWA	United Plant Guard Workers of America
UPI	United Press International
UPITN	United Press International independent Television News
UPIU	United Paperworkers International Union
UPS	Ultraviolet Photoemission Spectroscopy Uninterruptible Power System
UPU	Universal Postal Union

URI	Upper Respiratory Infection
URISA	Urban and Regional Information Systems Association
URR	Ultra-Rapid Reader
URSI	Union Radio-Scientifique Internationale (International Union of Radio Science)
URW	United Rubber, cork, linoleum and plastic Workers
US	Uniform System
USA	United Scenic Artists
	United States Army
	United States of America
USAC	United States Auto Club
USACC	United States Army Communications Command
USACE	United States Army Corps of Engineers
USAF	United States Aikido Federation
	United States Air Force
USAFI	United States Armed Forces Institute
USAGA	United States of America Goju Association
USAR	United States Army Reserve
USARSA	United States Amateur Roller Skating Association
USASA	United States Army Security Agency
USASI	United States of America Standards Institute
USBM	United States Bureau of Mines
USC	United States Code
	United States Customs
USCA	United States Code Annotated
USCC	United States Circuit Court
USCCR	United States Commission on Civil Rights
USCE	United States Corps of Engineers

USCF	United States Chess Federation United States Cycling Federation
USCG	United States Coast Guard
USCGS	United States Coast and Geodetic Survey
USCS	United States Customary System (Foot-Pound-Second)
USDA	United States Department of Agriculture
USDC	United States Department of Commerce
USDE	United States Department of Energy
USDI	United States Department of the Interior
USDJ	United States Department of Justice
USDL	United States Department of Labor
USDT	United States Department of Transportation
USES	United States Employment Service
USET	United States Equestrian Team
USFHA	United States Field Hockey Association
USFS	United States Forest Service
USFSA	United States Figure Skating Association
USFWS	United States Fish and Wildlife Service
USGA	United States Golf Association
USGF	United States Gymnastics Federation
USGS	United States Geological Survey
USHA	United States Handball Association
USIA	United States Information Agency
USIS	United States Information Service
USITA	United States Independent Telephone Association

USJA	United States Judo Association
USJF	United States Judo Federation
USLSA	United States League of Savings Associations
USLTA	Uniform Simplification of Land Transfers Act
	United States Lawn Tennis Association
JSM	UltraSonic Machining
	Underwater-to-Surface Missile
USMA	United States Military Academy
USMC	United States Marine Corps
USMM	United States Merchant Marine
USN	United States Navy
USNA	United States Naval Academy
USNR	United States Naval Reserve
USO	United Service Organization
USOC	United States Olympic Committee
USOE	United States Office of Education
USP	Uniform Specification Program
	U.S. Pharmacopeia
USPA	United States Parachute Association
	United States Polo Association
USPO	United States Patent Office
USPS	United States Postal Service
	United States Power Squadron (Boating)
USPSD	United States Political Science Documents
USR	United States supreme court Reports
USRA	United States Railway Association
	United States Revolver Association
USS	United States Sellers (Standard Threads)
	United States (Steamer) (Ship)
USSA	United States Ski Association
USSG	United States Standard Gage (Sheet, Plate, Iron and Steel)

USSI	United States Smithsonian Institution
USSR	Union of Soviet Socialist Republics
USTA	United States Tennis Association
	United States Trotting Association
USTC	United States Tax Court
USTCRD&WWA	United Slate, Tile and Composition, Roofers, Damp and Waterproof Workers Association
USTPA	United States Tennis Professionals Association
USTS	United States Travel Service
USTTA	United States Table Tennis Association
USVBA	United States Volley Ball Association
USW	Ultra-Short Wave
USWA	United Shoe Workers of America
	United Steel Workers of America
USWLA	United States Women's Lacrosse Association
USWMS	Uniform State Waterway Marking System
USYRU	United States Yacht Racing Union
UT	Utah
UTGC	Uniform Tire quality Grading
UTS	Ultimate Tensile Strength
UTU	United Transportation Union
UTW	Under The Wing (Plane Engine)
	United Telegraph Workers
UTWA	United Textile Workers of America
UV	Ultraviolet
	Under Voltage
UVC	Urban Volunteer Corps

U/W Underwater
UWA United Way of America
UWUA Utility Workers Union of
America

UXO UneXploded Ordnance

V Roman Numeral 5
Vanadium
Velocity
Volume
Volt
VA Veterans Administration
Virginia
VAC Volts Alternating Current
VACE Voice-Activated Computer
Exchange
VAD Vice ADmiral
VAM Virtual Access Method
VAMA Vinyl Acetate Maleic Acid
VANs Value Added Networks
VAR Vacuum-Arc Remelted (Steel)
Visual-Aural Range (Radio)
VASIS Visual Approach Slope Indicator
System
VAT Value-Added Tax
VAV Variable Air Volume (Heating)
VAWT Vertical-Axis Wind Turbine

VC Video Correlator
Viet Cong
Voltage Coefficient

VCB	Vertical Center of Buoyancy (Boat)
VCD	Variable-Capacitance Diode
VCG	Vector CardioGram
	Vertical Center of Gravity (Boat)
VCM	Vinyl Chloride Monomer
VCO	Voltage-Controlled Oscillator
VCP	Visual Comfort Probability (Building)
	Vitrified Clay Pipe
VCR	Video Cassette Recorder
	Voltage Coefficient Resistance
VD	Vapor Density
	Venereal Disease
VDC	Direct Current Volts
VDCW	Direct Current Working Volts
VDG	Venereal Disease-Gonorrhea
VDH	Valvular Disease of the Heart
VDR	Voltage-Dependent Resistor
VDRS	Vehicular Disc Reproduction System
VDS	Variable Depth Sonar
	Vehicle Detector Station
	Venereal Disease-Syphilis
VDT	Video Display Terminal
VE	Value Engineering
VEAP	Veterans Educational Assistance Program
VEB	Variable Elevation Beam (Antenna)
VECO	Vernier Engine Cut Off
VER	Visual Evoked Response
VES	Veterans Employment Service
VFAC	Variable Frequency Alternating Current
VFO	Variable Frequency Oscillator
VFR	Visual Flight Rules
VFW	Veterans of Foreign Wars
V-G	Variable Geometry

VGA	Variable Gain Amplifier	
VGC	Viscosity-Gravity Constant (Oil)	
VGLI	Veterans' Group Life Insurance	
VGPI	Visual Glide Path Indicator	
VH	Vickers Hardness	271
	Viral Hepatitis	
VHB	Very Heavy Bomber	VGA-VLI
VHD	Valvular Heart Disease	
VHF	Very High Frequency	
VHS	Video Home System	
VHSI	Very High Speed Integration	
VHSIC	Very High Speed Integrated Circuit	
VI	Virgin Islands	
	Viscosity Index	
VID	Vehicle IDentification	
VIN	Vehicle Identification Number	
VIP	Variable Information Processing	
	Very Important (People) (Person)	
VIR	Valve In Receiver	
	Vertical Interval Reference (TV)	
VISAM	Virtual Indexed Sequential Access Method	
VISSR	Visible Infrared Spin-Scan Radiometer	
VISTA	Volunteers In Service To America	
VITA	Volunteers for International Technical Assistance	
VK	View in Kilometers	
VLA	Very Long Array	
VLB	Very Long Baseline	
VLBI	Very Long Baseline Interferometry (Polar)	
VLCC	Very Large Crude Carrier	
VLDL	Very Light Density Lipoprotein	
VLF	Very Low Frequency	
VLI	Variable Life Insurance	

VLR	Very Long Range
VLS	Vapor-Liquid-Solid
VLSI	Very Large Scale Integration
VM	View in Miles
	Virtual Memory (Computer)
	Volatile Matter (Coal)
VMA	Valve Manufacturers Association
	Voids in Mineral Aggregate
VMC	Visual Meteorological Conditions
VMDP	Veterinary Medical Data Program
VMOS	Vertical-grooved Metal-Oxide-Silicon
VMP	Vertically Moored Platform (Drilling)
VM&P	Varnish Makers and Painters
VMS	Vehicle Maintenance System
VMT	Vehicle Miles of Travel
VNA	Visiting Nurse Association
VNC	Voice Numerical Control
VNL	Via Net Loss (Transmission)
VNLF	Via Net Loss Factor
VO	Voice Over
VOA	Voice Of America
VOD	Vacuum-Oxygen Decarburization
VOM	Volt-Ohmm Milliammeter
VOR	Very high frequency Omni-directional Radio range
VOX	VOice activated (Telephone, Radio)
VP	Vanishing Point (Drafting)
	Vapor Pressure
	Vice President
VPI	Vapor Phase Inhibitor
V-R	Voltage-Regulator

VRI	Virus Respiratory Infection
VRT	Voltage Regulator Tube
VS	Valve Slide-wire
	Vital Sign
VSB	Vestigial Side Band (Radio)
VSCC	Vintage Sports Car Club
VSE	Vacuum System Engineer
	Virtual Storage Extended
	(Computer)
VSI	Vertical Scale Indicator
VSLI	Veteran Special Life Insurance
VSR	Very Short Range (Radar)
VST	Very Small Truck
V-STOL	Vertical and Short TakeOff and
	Landing
VSV	Vacuum Switching Valve
VSWR	Voltage Standing-Wave Ratio
	(Radio)
VT	Variable Thrust
	Variable Time (Fuse)
	Vermont
V&T	Volume and Tension (Pulse)
VTAM	Vortex Telecommunications
	Access Method
VTF	Vertical Tracking Force (Stereo)
VTOL	Vertical TakeOff and Landing
VTR	Video Tape Recorder
VTTA	Veterans Time Trial Association
	(Bicycling)
VTVM	Vacuum-Tube VoltMeter
VU	Volt Unit (Electric Wave)
VW	Volkswagen

W	Watt
	West
WA	Washington
WAAC	Women's Auxiliary Army Corps
WAAF	Women's Auxiliary Air Force
WAAM	Wide Area Antiarmor Munitions
WAC	Women's Army Corps
	Working Alternating Current
WAD	Wide Area Dialing (Telephone)
WADS	Wide Area Data Service
WAE	When Actually Employed
WAF	Women in the Air Force
WAM	Women And Mathematics
WAMTMC	Western Area Military Traffic Management Command (Army)
WAO	Wet Air Oxidation
WARC	World Administrative Radio Conference
WAS	Waste Activated Sludge
WASP	White Anglo-Saxon Protestant
	Women's Airforces Service Pilots
WATS	Wide Area Telephone Service

WAVES	Women Appointed for Volunteer Emergency Service (Naval Reserve)
Wb	Weber (Magnetic Flux)
WB	Water-Borne (Coatings)
	Wingback (Football)
WBA	World Boxing Association
WBBG	World Body Building Guild
WBC	White Blood Cells
	World Boxing Council
WC	Water Closet
WCA	World Calendar Association
WCC	Women's College Coalition
	World Council of Churches
WCF	Winchester Center Fire (Rifle)
	Women's Campaign Fund
WCG	Worldwide Church of God
WCT	World Championship Tennis
WCTU	Woman's Christian Temperance Union
WDC	Working Direct Current
WDDA	Wholesale Demand Deposit Accounting
WEEAP	Women's Educational Equity Act Program
WESTPO	WESTern governors' Policy Office
WEU	Western Europe Union
WF	Weatherproof Faience (Tile)
	Won on Foul (Boxing)
WFAOSB	World Food and Agricultural Outlook and Situation Board
WFM	Weatherproof Faience Mosaics
WFTU	World Federation of Trade Unions
WG	Wine Gallon

WGA Writers Guild of America

WHA World Hockey Association
WHO World Health Organization

WI Wisconsin
    Wrought Iron
WIA Water-Insoluble fatty Acids
    Wounded In Action
WIBC Women's International Bowling
    Congress
WIG Wing-In-Ground (Plane)
WIIR Water-Insoluble Inorganic
    Residue
WIN Work INcentive
    Workshop In Nonviolence

WINO Wine Investigation for Novices
    and Oenophiles
WIPO World Intellectual Property
    Organization
WISE Worldwide Information System
    for Engineering
WITS Worldwide Information and
    Trade Systems

WL Water Line

WM Wattmeter
    Wire Mesh (Fence)
WMAB Weather Modification Advisory
    Board
WMO World Meteorological
    Organization
WMS Work Measurement Sampling

WNL Within Normál Limits (Medical)

WO Warrant Officer
    Work Order
W/O Without
WOAC Warrant Officer Advanced
    Course

WOG	Water, Oil or Gas (Non-Shock Valve)
WP	Warsaw Pact
	Water Potential
	White Phosphorous (Ammunition)
	Word Processing
WPA	Works Projects Administration
WPC	Watts Per Candlepower
WPCF	Water Pollution Control Foundation
WPGA	Women's Professional Golfers' Association
WPGT	Women's Professional Golf Tour
WPI	Wholesale Price Index
WPKO	World Professional Karate Organization
wpm	Words Per Minute
WPMA	Word Processing Management Association
WPS	Widowed Persons Service
WPSL	Women's Professional Softball League
WR	Wasserman Reaction
	Wide Receiver (Football)
	World Record
WRC	Water Resources Council
	World Relief Commission
WRU	Who aRe yoU (Telex)
WRWP	Water-Repellent Wood Preservative
WSCS	World Stamp Collector's Society
WSD	Working Stress Design (Steel)
WSP	Work Systems Package (Navy Underwater Salvage)
WTA	Women's Tennis Association
WTC	World Trade Center
WTDR	World Traders Data Report
WTG	Wind Turbine Generator

WTT World Team Tennis

WU Western Union
WUX Western Union telegram
WV West Virginia

WW Wire-Wound
WWA Western Writers of America
WWB Wet Weight Basis (Drying)
WWEMA Water and Wastewater Equipment Manufacturers Association
WWG Warrington Wire Gage
WWM-CCS WorldWide Military Command and Control System (Wimex)
WWPBA Western Women's Professional Bowlers Association
WWW World Weather Watch

Wx Weather
WY Wyoming

X Cross
Experimental
Roman Numeral 10

Xe Xenon

XL Existing Light (Camera)
Extra Large

XP Xeroderma Pigmentosum (Skin
Disease)

XU X-ray Unit

Y

Y	Yttrium
YACC	Youth Adult Conservation Corps
YAG	Yttrium-Aluminum-Garnet
Yb	Ytterbium
YBA	Youth Basketball Association
YCS	Youth Community Service
yd	Yard
YETP	Youth Employment and Training Program
YFC	Youth For Christ
YFD	Yard Floating Dock
YIG	Yttrium-Iron-Garnet
YMCA	Young Men's Christian Association
YMF	Young Musicians Foundation
YO	Yard Oiler (Navy Ship)

YRT Yearly Renewable Term
(Insurance)

YSB Yacht Safety Bureau

YT Yard Tug
YTD Year To Date

YWCA Young Women's Christian
Association

ZANLA Zimbabwe African National
Liberation Army
ZANU Zimbabwe African National
Union
ZAPU Zimbabwe African Peoples
Union

ZBB Zero Based Budgeting

ZD Zenith Distance (Navigation)
Zero Defects
ZDBT Zinc DiBenzyldiThiocarbamate

ZEG Zero Economic Growth
ZETA Zero Energy Thermonuclear
Assembly

ZFB Signals Fading Badly

ZI Zone of Interior
ZIP Zone Improvement Plan (Post
Office)
ZIPRA Zimbabwe African Peoples
Union (Rhodesia)

ZMAR Zeus Multifunction Array Radar

Zn Zinc

ZPC Zero Point of Charge
ZPG Zero Population Growth

Zr Zirconium

ZST Zone Standard Time

ZT Zone Time

ZUM Zone Usage Measurement
(Telephone)

423
PAR

Parks, Betsy M.

The dictionary of
initials

DATE			